The Book of

£2·50

1. The Royal Standard

2. Union Flag

Plate I

VICE-ADMIRAL GORDON CAMPBELL VC., DSO
AND I. O. EVANS FRGS

The Book of Flags

Seventh Edition

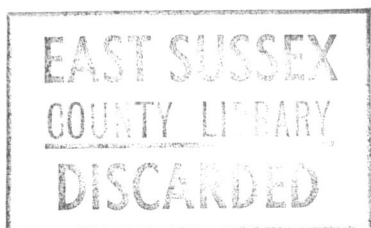

London
OXFORD UNIVERSITY PRESS
1974

Oxford University Press, Ely House, London W. 1

GLASGOW NEW YORK TORONTO MELBOURNE WELLINGTON
CAPE TOWN IBADAN NAIROBI DAR ES SALAAM LUSAKA ADDIS ABABA
DELHI BOMBAY CALCUTTA MADRAS KARACHI LAHORE DACCA
KUALA LUMPUR SINGAPORE HONG KONG TOKYO

ISBN 0 19 273132 7

First published 1950
Second Edition 1953
Third Edition 1957
Fourth Edition 1960
Fifth Edition 1965
Revised Edition 1966
Sixth Edition 1969
Seventh Edition 1974

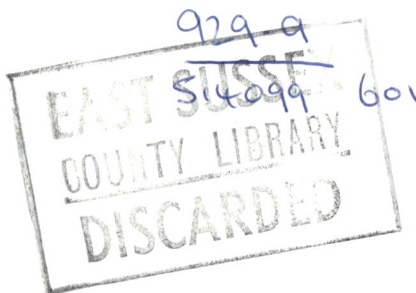

ERRATUM

The Publisher apologises for the fact that owing to a Printer's error the flag for Indiana has been printed upside down.

PRINTED IN GREAT BRITAIN BY
MORRISON AND GIBB LTD., LONDON AND EDINBURGH

Preface

I STARTED to compile this book in 1938 and had hoped to complete it by the end of 1939—but after collecting a great deal of material I found myself back in uniform and my very able secretary, Miss Mackay Houston, blossomed forth as a W.R.N.S. officer. By the time the war was over great changes had taken place, not only in Royal and National Flags but also in domestic ones. Thrones had fallen. Dictators had been liquidated and even the flags of the British Empire were changing daily. It was obvious that practically a new book would be needed: but by this time I had anchored in a village away from the facilities required.

I therefore invited Mr. I. O. Evans to collaborate with me; this he kindly agreed to do and the work appears under our joint names.

GORDON CAMPBELL
August 15, 1949

Preface to the Seventh Edition

SINCE this book was first published in 1950, the many changes in the world's flags have demanded its repeated revision. While still remaining within the Commonwealth, for example, many of Britain's former colonies have now achieved independence, and these signify their new status by using their own flags instead of being represented by badges upon the Ensigns. Others, the Republic of South Africa and Pakistan, have withdrawn from the Commonwealth.

Because of these and other developments it has been decided to discontinue giving separate treatment to the Commonwealth Countries, and to group all the regions except the British Isles and the United States in geographical order.

Notwithstanding this and other changes, however, *The Book of Flags* still retains the character originally impressed upon it by the late Admiral Gordon Campbell, so that the work which he had inspired and directed remains a tribute to his memory.

I. O. EVANS
August 7th, 1973

Acknowledgements

The thanks of the authors are due to:

Sir Gerald Wollaston, former Garter King of Arms.
Sir Francis Grant, former Lord Lyon King of Arms.
W. J. G. Verco, Esq., M.V.O., Norroy and Ulster King of Arms, and Earl
  Marshal's Secretary.
Lieutenant-Commander R. S. Bryden, R.N.
Wing Commander T. R. N. Wheatley-Smith, Ministry of Defence.
H. H. Thomas, Esq., Keeper of Records, Guildhall, London.
D. Bonner-Smith, Esq., F.R.Hist.S.
H. Gresham Carr, Esq., F.R.G.S.
C. V. Hill, Esq.
The Secretary and staff, Royal Geographical Society.
The Director, The Manx Museum, Douglas, Isle of Man.
The Information Officer, the London Information Centre, United Nations.
The Controller, H.M. Stationery Office.
Mrs. Mackay Mure.
The Archdeacon and the Chapter Office of Westminster.
The Ministry of Public Building and Works.
The British European Airways Corporation.
The British Overseas Airways Corporation.
The Flag Research Center, Winchester, Mass., U.S.A.
The Flag Section of the Heraldry Society.
The Flag Institute.

Also the Secretaries and Officers of various Embassies, Legations,
Dominion and Colonial Offices, and other public bodies, and the Directors
and staff of various Shipping, Shipbuilding and other Companies.

Contents

Gordon Campbell

BORN in 1886, into a well-known Scottish family, Gordon Campbell quickly followed its tradition of service in the Forces. At fourteen he entered the Royal Navy, and two years later became a midshipman in H.M.S. *Prince George*. He served in a light cruiser in the Pacific; then, as a sub-lieutenant, in the destroyer H.M.S. *Arun* with the Channel Fleet; in 1913 his first command was H.M.S. *Bittern*.

In the First World War he commanded the converted tramp-steamer *Q5*, one of the 'Mystery Ships' whose task it was to lure enemy submarines to destruction. Ingeniously disguised and with her guns camouflaged, she would allow a submarine to attack her, send off a 'panic party' in boats as though they meant to abandon her—then lower the Red Ensign of the Merchant Service and hoist the Royal Navy's White Ensign as she opened fire.

In 1916 the *Q5* sank her first submarine, later damaging another and hunting yet another out of British waters. In 1917 she was torpedoed by a German U-Boat. Though crippled and sinking, she bided her time until the 'panic party' had lured the enemy vessel within range, and then sank her. She was towed to safety and beached, and her Commander was awarded the Victoria Cross.

The last of his Mystery Ships—the *Dunraven*—fought on for hours while not merely crippled and sinking but actually on fire with her ammunition exploding piecemeal.

Gordon Campbell, now a Captain, was transferred to the light cruisers and in 1918 he commanded a flotilla of destroyers.

Retired in 1928 with the rank of Vice-Admiral, he lectured and wrote two books, *My Mystery Ships*, describing his work in the Royal Navy, and *Number Thirteen*, his autobiography. In 1931 he entered Parliament as a member of the National Government and spoke on Naval affairs. Later he wrote a life of the explorer Captain Cook, several factual narratives of adventure at sea, and some exciting fictional stories of life in the Royal Navy.

He died in 1953, having throughout his life upheld in courage, in public spirit and in generosity the splendid traditions of the Service in which he had played so distinguished a part.

List of Colour Plates

The following books have been consulted:

Flags of All Nations, and its supplements (Admiralty)
Flags of the World Past and Present by V. Wheeler-Holohan
National Flags by E. H. Baxter
Sea Flags by Commander Hilary P. Mead
British Flags by W. G. Perrin
How to Learn the International Code published by Brown, Son & Ferguson
House Flags and Funnels of British and Foreign Shipping Companies by Paymaster-Lieutenant E. C. Talbot-Booth, R.N.R.
State Names, Flags, Seals, Songs, Birds, Flowers, and other Symbols by G. E. Shankle
The Flag of the United States by M. M. Quaife

In the Revisions the following have also been consulted:

Flags of All Nations, 1955 and 1958 editions and their supplements (Admiralty)
Flags of the World edited by H. Gresham Carr, F.R.G.S., revised by E. M. C. Barraclough
Flags over South Africa by R. Gerard
Flags, Funnels and Hull Colours by Colin Stewart, revised by John S. Styring
Yacht Flags and Ensigns by E. M. C. Barraclough
Flags for Ship Modellers and Marine Artists by Alec A. Purves
The Colour of Chivalry by H. B. Pereira
Standards, Guidons and Colours of the Commonwealth Forces by Major I. J. Edwards
Colours and Standards in the Royal Air Force (H.M. Stationery Office)
The Flag Bulletin of the Flag Research Center
The Flag of Stars by Frank Cayley
The Flag Book of the United States by Whitney Smith
Flagmaster

Introduction

FLAGS are as old as civilization, yet they still retain their ancient power. Throughout history men have realized that they could express their feelings for their country and its people, their loyalty and sense of patriotic duty, by showing respect for their emblem, the national flag, and by understanding something of its meaning and history. This helped them to be fellow-citizens of a community instead of merely being people who happened to live together in one part of the earth. This is as true today as ever it was: we need to respect not only our own flags but those of other nations, and to understand their meaning.

We all realize this in moments of crisis. During the Battle of Britain a heartening custom prevailed: when a house was destroyed, the survivors hastened to hoist a Union Flag over the ruins. How better could they express their courage, their undaunted spirit in the midst of disaster, their defiance of the enemy, their stern determination never to yield?

On Victory Day we delighted to decorate our homes with the flags of the Allied Nations. It paid a tribute to them and to our cause and expressed our rejoicing as nothing else could do; for flags, like words, are a means of explaining our ideas; and like words they can be badly misused. Ignorance of their use made some people say with their flags the exact opposite of what they meant. During the Victory celebrations one or two people unintentionally paid tribute to their conquered foes by displaying those nations' flags, and in both the celebrations and the blitz many people turned their flag into a sign of distress instead of triumph or defiance by hoisting it upside-down.

Already flags of Soviet Russia have been scattered on the moon, and since 1969 the Stars and Stripes has been several times raised above its surface by the crews of the *Apollo* space-ships. Special pennants have also been sent to Venus by the U.S.S.R.

The designs on flags were chosen not at random but because of their meaning. Some were deliberately selected in recent times; others have been in use from time immemorial, their origin coming from ancient legends or being completely lost in the past. To interpret the meaning of a flag helps us to understand and appreciate something of the history and ideals of the country which flies it. A knowledge of flags helps us to be better citizens not only of our own islands, but of the British Commonwealth of Nations and of the world.

The Personal Flag of
Queen Elizabeth II

The Personal Flag of Charles, Prince of Wales,
for use during his visits to the Principality

1

FLAGS AND THEIR MEANING

A great street paved with water, filled with shipping,
And all the world's flags flying and seagulls dipping.

JOHN MASEFIELD: OF THE THAMES

SINCE the dawn of history groups of people have represented themselves by animal or other designs. Perhaps the oldest pictures in the world are the animals which prehistoric artists painted on cave-walls in Southern France and Northern Spain maybe twenty thousand years ago. We do not know what these designs meant, but they may represent *totems*, the sacred animals of ancient tribes. A bison drawn rearing on its hind legs certainly looks rather like one of the *supporters* which heralds place on coats of arms.

When weaving and dyeing were discovered—probably in ancient Egypt many centuries ago—they gave a new and very striking way of displaying such emblems. A piece of coloured cloth fluttering in the breeze is not merely beautiful but impressive and stirring. It seems almost as if it were alive: birds painted on it appear to be flying, animals appear to be roaming the forests or aggressively pawing the air. The peoples of ancient civilizations used streamers along with, or instead of, the images and other badges which they bore ceremonially on poles. The Roman auxiliaries had their Dragon banner, the Saxons had their White Horse, the Vikings their Raven flag.

Many such emblems had a religious meaning, and this custom continued when Europe became Christian. Nowadays banners showing pictures of the Saints and of religious symbols are carried only in solemn church processions, round the streets in various countries, and along the aisles of churches in our own land. In the Middle Ages they were actually taken into battle. 'The Battle of the Standards', so called because it was waged round a cross and three Saints' banners, was not the only occasion on which such emblems served as rallying-points. Similar banners flew side by side with the Royal Standard of King Henry V at the Battle of Agincourt.

In the Middle Ages the designing of flags was a branch of heraldry. All the rulers in Europe had their heralds, whose duty it was—and may still be—not only to make proclamations on their behalf but to record the family history of people of rank and to prepare their coat of arms and other emblems. Although so ancient, heraldry has always kept up to date: there is even a coat of arms for the Atomic Energy Authority. England and Scotland each has its College of Arms under officers with the traditional titles of Garter and Lyon Kings of Arms.

Throughout Europe the Colleges of Arms worked in co-operation, using

1

special technical terms which all heralds could understand and drawing up rules they all must obey. Heraldry in our islands uses a strange blend of English with Norman-French words, some similar to modern French and others quite different: it speaks of green as *vert* but calls red not *rouge* but *gules*; this may be an Arabic word, meaning 'rose', brought to Europe by the Crusaders. Even some of its English words are used with special meanings: the background of a flag, on which its designs appear, is called its *field*.

British heralds recognize only five colours, *azure*, *gules*, *sable*, *vert*, and *purpure* (blue, red, black, green, and purple). Abroad orange is also recog-

THE SHADING USED IN THIS BOOK TO INDICATE THE DIFFERENT COLOURS

  Yellow   White   Blue

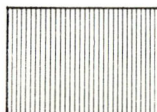   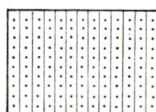

 Red   Black   Green   Brown

  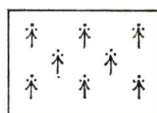

  Purple   Orange   Ermine

nized under the name of *tenné*. They do not regard yellow and white as 'colours' at all, but speak of them the two 'metals', *or* and *argent* (gold and silver)—even when they consist of cloth! They also use a number of 'furs', such as *ermine* (white with black markings), but except in royal standards these very seldom appear in flags.

One of the strictest rules of heraldry is that metal must never be placed on metal nor colour on colour. Whether on a coat of arms or on a flag, no two heraldic colours must ever touch: they must be separated by a strip, however narrow (the heralds call it a *fimbriation*), of one of the heraldic metals, yellow or white. Similarly these two metals must never touch: they must be separated by a narrow strip of one of the colours.

This explains why so many of the older tricolour flags consist of white or yellow between two heraldic colours, and why our own Union Flag bears a fimbriation separating the red from the blue, much narrower than the broad white stripe of St. Andrew's Cross. Many of the more modern flags, however, disregard the rule by placing two colours or metals side by side. Readers may be interested to notice which of the flags illustrated in this book are correct heraldically and which are not.

Flags meant to be flown at sea or over lofty buildings have, of course, to be far stronger than the cotton ones used to ornament houses or the delicate regimental colours made of embroidered silk which the Army carries on ceremonial parades. Such flags are traditionally made of *bunting*, a strong woollen cloth woven in Yorkshire, which was formerly made in strips forty yards long and nine inches wide. The bunting at present being used in the Royal Navy for flag-making, however, is a nylon-worsted material which is purchased in rolls thirty-eight inches wide. The old method of stating the size of the flag—that it is so many nine-inch 'breadths' —is still retained (thus a 'four breadths' flag is three feet wide). Most of the flags are made in the Dockyard Sail Lofts by stitching the material together, but any heraldic details or badges are obtained from the trade and sewn on. Small flags up to three breadths (twenty-seven inches wide), including car flags, are also bought from the trade and are dye-printed.

The flags used in the Royal Navy are sewn on to pieces of stout rope, ending in two metal clips, one just above the flag, the other about a foot below. As they can easily be clipped together, these *Inglefield clips* (so called after the inventor in about 1890) enable the flag to be bent on to the halliards, even hurriedly and in a bad light, without any risk of its being hoisted upside-down.

The part of a flag nearest the halliards is called the *hoist* and the part farther away the *fly*. The upper half of the hoist is the *first quarter* of the flag, the upper half of the fly is its second quarter; the lower halves of hoist and fly are its third and fourth quarters, and this is their order of heraldic importance. The quarters are sometimes called *cantons*, from an old French word meaning 'corners'. The canton is, however, the first quarter; this is the place of honour in a flag and, as in our naval ensigns, may contain a special design—a flag within a flag. The ensigns and flags may be *defaced*, as the heralds call it, by a distinguishing badge or *charge*. A long tapering flag is a *pendant* (pronounced, and sometimes spelled, 'pennant').

Whether a flag conforms to the heraldic rules or not, it needs to be easily distinguishable from others and to have a striking design. Words are seldom used on flags; they are difficult to read when waving in the breeze or sagging during a lull, and even when legible they are neither impressive nor heraldic. Small details of design are equally hard to distinguish: bold patterns of contrasting colour are most easily recognized.

Flags convey a meaning not only by their pattern but by their position. This has produced phrases used in everyday life. If a political speaker says that his opponents have 'struck their flag', but that his own party have 'nailed their colours to the mast', his audience may or may not agree with him, but they all know what he means.

Ships are said to fly or *wear* a flag, this second expression generally referring to the personal standards, flags, or other emblems of individuals. The *ensign* of a ship is usually flown on a staff in the stern (the *ensign staff*) or on a gaff, and some British and foreign ensigns have special emblems in the canton. The *jack* is generally flown on a staff in the bows (the *jackstaff*). A flag hoisted at the mast-head may be in a compact roll with a coil of the halliard knotted round it so that a sharp tug on this will break the flag out when required.

The heraldic flags used in the Middle Ages differed greatly from those of today. A square or oblong flag was then called not a standard but a *banner*; its size depended on its owner's rank. In England, the *standard* bore a St. George's Cross in its hoist, and in Scotland a St. Andrew's Cross; its fly, which was rounded and divided at the tip, tapered and bore its owner's family colours and crest; a somewhat similar flag was used by Captain Scott when he reached the South Pole.

The flag of a 'Knight Bachelor' was the *pennon*, which had swallow-tails; to honour a deed of valour on the battlefield the king might cut off the swallow-tails, converting the pennon into a small banner and promoting its owner to a 'Knight Banneret' or—as we say nowadays—a Baronet. The Squire's flag was a *pennoncel*, tapering to a point. The *streamer*, which also tapered, and the *banderole*, which had parallel edges, were very long and narrow. The earliest type of *gonfalon* hung from a horizontal crossbar.

To fly a flag at *half-mast* is a recognized sign of mourning: it is not raised to that position direct but is hoisted mast-head high and immediately lowered. The flag is half-masted to an officer or rating who has died while on the active list and whose body is committed to the sea or buried within the precincts of a naval port or place where the ship is lying. On the death of a member of the Royal Family or of the ruler of a friendly state, flags are lowered to half-mast, both on sea and on land, as a sign of the nation's grief.

By custom and as an act of courtesy, merchant ships lower their colours to warships. The colour is re-hoisted when the warship has returned such salute; this is plainly more convenient than the old sailing-ship custom of lowering the topsails. To *strike* the flag is to lower it and not re-hoist it: this is the recognized sign of surrender. To wear one national flag over another is a sign of victory in war; in peace it is a deliberate insult to the country which the lower flag represents—people who decorate their homes with assorted national colours would do well to remember this! To honour a flag of a friendly nation without belittling one's own, the two should be of equal size and should be flown at the same height side by side.

The earliest book of flags of which we know was compiled not by a herald but by a monk. 'The Book of all the Knowledge of all the Kingdoms,

Lords, and Lordships in the World' describes the travels of a Catalan Franciscan monk who lived in the fourteenth century but whose name is not known. It is illustrated with the arms and flags and other heraldic devices of the countries he visited.

In modern times, official flag-books are sometimes issued by the naval authorities of the different nations; they are very full and comprehensive and are from time to time modernized by the issue of supplements. Even these do not bring them completely up to date, however, for by the time the supplements have been published there have been further changes. The official book of the British Admiralty is *Flags of All Nations*.

The Book of Flags aims not at completeness but at describing the more notable and interesting flags. Heraldry, to which flags are related, has been called the 'shorthand of history', and we need to know something of history if we are to understand the world in which we live. Here, then, are some of history's shorthand notes.

2

THE ROYAL STANDARD

To say with heart and voice:
God save the Queen.

THE BRITISH NATIONAL ANTHEM

EVERY Londoner knows the Royal Standard: flying over Buckingham Palace it shows that Her Majesty the Queen is in residence. Its rich heraldic colours of red, gold, and blue, and the graceful curves of its design—the three lions, the rampant lion, and the harp—distinguish it unmistakably from the plainer red, white, and blue, and the straight lines of our other flags.

Its design is the Royal Coat of Arms, which also appears on government documents and used to appear on some British coins. This makes the Standard the Queen's official banner which none of her subjects should fly. When she enters a building—even if it be, say, the grandstand at the Derby— the Royal Standard is at once raised above it; as she boards a ship, the Standard is broken at the mast-head.

The Royal Standard is never flown at half-mast as a sign of mourning, for it is the law that 'the Crown' never dies; one reign follows continuously after another. 'The King is dead', the Heralds make the sad announcement; but at once they follow it with the proclamation: 'Long live the King!' Or, as in 1952, 'Long live the Queen!'

There are a few exceptions to the rule that the Royal Standard marks the Queen's actual presence. When it flies over Westminster Abbey, it need not mean that she is attending a service. King Edward VII granted the Abbey the privilege of flying the Standard when the Sovereign is in its neighbourhood—when, for example, she is present at the opening of Parliament.

At one time the Standard was worn by the Lord High Admiral, when afloat, as representative of the Crown. It used also to be hoisted over ships of the Royal Navy on the Sovereign's Birthday and other state occasions, but this custom has likewise ceased.

If the Queen appoints a member of her family to represent her—for example, on a state visit abroad—she may authorize him to fly not the Royal Standard but his own personal standard.

The design of the Royal Standard has changed greatly through the centuries, but one emblem has long formed part of it. The use of one, two, or three, lions—they may be leopards—as the Arms of the King of England dates back to Richard the Lion-heart, if not to William the Conqueror.

King Edward III added another emblem: he wanted to represent on his flag his claim to the throne of France. He may, indeed, have considered France the most important part of his kingdom, for he gave its emblem the place of honour in the first quarter of the flag. He also placed it in the fourth, leaving the second and third quarters for the three lions of England.

The French royal emblem was the heraldic lily, the fleur-de-lis. The flag of the French king was at that time *powdered*, as the heralds call it, with lilies, some of them in halves on its edge, so that it looked like a piece cut from a larger sheet of tapestry. This arrangement was also adopted in King Edward's flag (Plate II, figure 1).

The French king later greatly improved the appearance of his flag by reducing its lilies to three, complete and arranged in a triangle. Henry IV accordingly copied this alteration on the English Royal Standard, to show that he claimed France as it then was and not as it had been (Plate II, figure 2). His standard, in which the French lilies were quartered with the English lion, remained in use until the marriage of Queen Mary to Philip of Spain. In accordance with the heraldic rules she then *impaled* her husband's and her own arms by placing them side by side on the one flag, the husband's taking the position of honour in the hoist.

Queen Elizabeth I restored the plain Henry IV Standard. This explains two perplexing lines in Lord Macaulay's poem *The Armada*. In the upper part of the flag the lilies were just in front of the three lions, which would seem to move as the flag fluttered:

> *Look how the lion of the sea lifts up his ancient crown*
> *And underneath his deadly paw treads the gay lilies down.*

When King James VI of Scotland became King James I of England, with a claim also to be King of France, he naturally wished to show both kingdoms on his flag. Since at least the thirteenth century the Royal Banner of the King of Scots had been the emblem previously used by King William the Lion: a lion rampant (standing erect as though about to fight). It was surrounded by a double framework, called a *tressure*, ornamented with heraldic lilies, a token perhaps of the ancient friendship between France and Scotland; this, like the lion, was red on a gold field. James placed this Scottish emblem in the second quarter of his flag, while in the third quarter he placed that of Ireland, which he also claimed to rule. This had been chosen by Henry VIII and was a gold harp with silver strings on a blue field.

King James' Standard was, however, very different from that of today. Though its second and third quarters were those we know so well, its first and fourth quarters included the *whole* of the English Royal Standard. The Lilies of France and the Lions of England thus appeared four times on divisions each one-sixteenth of the whole flag and one-quarter the size of those of Scotland and Ireland (Plate II, figure 3).

The new banner displeased the Scots, who claimed that their emblem should have the place of honour in the first quarter. The Royal Coat of Arms used in Scotland is indeed almost the reverse of the English, placing the Rampant Lion of Scotland in the first and fourth quarters and the Lions of England in the second. Nevertheless the Queen, when resident in Scotland, flies what the Scots call the 'English version' of her flag. She could instead fly the Rampant Lion and Tressure, for this is still in itself a Royal Standard. Its use by Scottish citizens is quite irregular; but the Queen's representatives, the Secretary of State for Scotland and the High Commissioner for the General Assembly, are authorized to fly it on official occasions.

The Royal Standard, of course, went out of use during the Commonwealth, its place being taken by the Protector's Standard. One Commonwealth naval flag contained the St. George's Cross in its first and fourth quarters, the St. Andrew's Saltire in the second, and the Irish harp in the third. On the centre of this rather unattractive-looking flag was placed a small shield bearing Cromwell's personal arms, a white lion on black.

On coming to the throne Charles II restored the James Standard. (During his return to England, however, as no Standard was available, the ship on which he sailed wore a Union Flag, bearing the Royal Crown and the initials 'C.R.' in gold.) The same Standard was also flown by James II, but after his abdication it was doubled. William III and Mary, who succeeded him, were joint sovereigns, and their Standard therefore bore their arms impaled—side by side—on one flag. (Both were Stuarts and so flew the James Standard.) Those of William, which were in the hoist, bore his father's arms, the rampant Lion of Nassau, gold on blue, on a small shield at the centre; those of Mary, in the fly, consisted simply of the James arms, and were disused after her death (Plate II, figure 4).

When England and Scotland were merged into Great Britain, Queen Anne symbolized this on the James flag which she had hitherto flown. The English lions and the Scottish lion rampant, which kept only about half its tressure, were impaled in the first and fourth quarters. The Irish harp remained in the third quarter. But the French lilies lost the place of honour in the first quarter and were relegated to the second, perhaps because the English ruler's claim to the throne of France was ceasing to appear valid (Plate II, figure 5).

George I removed the arms of Great Britain from the fourth quarter of Queen Anne's flag, of course leaving them in the first quarter, and substituted those of Hanover, of which he was Elector. This was a threefold state; its arms included two golden lions on red for Brunswick, another blue lion on gold for Luneburg, and a white horse for Westphalia. At its centre was the Crown of Charlemagne which showed the ruler's rank (Plate II, figure 6).

When the United Kingdom of Great Britain and Ireland was formed,

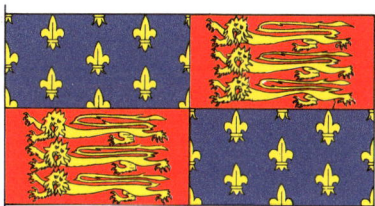

1. Standard of Edward III

2. Standard of Henry IV

3. Standard of James I

4. Standard of William III

5. Standard of Queen Anne

6. Standard of George I

7. Standard of George III

8. Standard of Prince of Wales

Plate II

it seemed incorrect to give as much space to Ireland as to England and Scotland put together. George III accordingly made further changes in the Standard. He placed the Lions of England in the first and fourth quarters, and the Rampant Lion and Tressure of Scotland in the second, leaving the Harp of Ireland in the third. The Arms of Hanover went on a large shield at the centre of the flag, with an 'Electoral Cap', later replaced by a Royal Crown, above it (Plate II, figure 7). The Lilies of France no longer appeared on the Royal Standard, George III having formally renounced all claim to the French throne.

The flag had in its many changes included emblems of the four countries which have at different times been England's most dangerous foes: France, Spain, and parts of Holland and Germany. The designs of the historic Royal Standard, Plate II, figures 1 to 7, are correct except that as flown the flags were shorter in proportion to their width.

The 'Salic law' in force on the Continent forbade Hanover to be ruled by a woman, and when Queen Victoria came to the throne the arms of that state vanished from her Royal Standard. This now represented only the four countries of the United Kingdom, Wales being regarded as part of England. Except for a few changes of detail introduced more recently, it had indeed come into its present form (Frontispiece, figure 1), its heraldic description being:

Quarterly. First and fourth *gules*, three lions passant guardant in pale *or* (England); second *or*, a lion rampant within a double tressure flory counter-flory *gules* (Scotland); third *azure*, a harp *or*, stringed *argent* (Ireland).

Passant guardant is heraldic for 'in a walking attitude from right to left with the front paw raised but the head turned full-face'; *in pale* means not that the gold colour of the lions is faint, but that they are arranged one vertically above the other; *flory and counterflory* means that the frame round the rampant lion is ornamented with flowers (heraldic lilies) both inside and out.

In 1960 Queen Elizabeth II decided to adopt a new Personal Flag. It was not intended that this should supplant the Royal Standard; it is to be used chiefly in Commonwealth countries such as India where the heraldic devices of the United Kingdom have no historic significance. The Flag, which is fringed with gold, consists of the initial letter 'E' ensigned with the Royal Crown, the whole within a chaplet of roses, all gold on a blue field (see page xii).

The Queen also has special Personal Flags for use in certain regions of the Commonwealth. In these the device used on her Personal Flag is depicted centrally on fields consisting of the arms of the respective countries. (See pages 60, 69, 70, 72–73, 77–78, 93, 97, 100, 101.)

In the first quarter of the standard of Prince Philip, Duke of Edinburgh, are three blue lions with golden crowns on a gold field ornamented with red hearts (Denmark); in the second a white cross on a blue field (Greece); the third two black pallets (vertical bars) on a white field (Mountbatten); and the fourth, also on a white field, a black castle on a rock proper (Edinburgh).

Several members of the Royal Family have Personal Standards bearing their coats of arms. The heraldic tradition still maintains that a queen impales her arms on her flag with those of her husband. The Standard of a Queen, the wife of a King of England, accordingly bears the Royal Standard in its hoist.

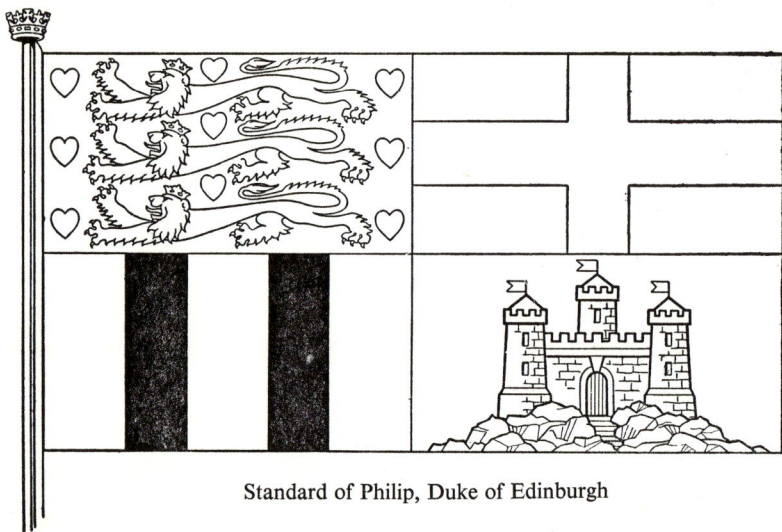

Standard of Philip, Duke of Edinburgh

The arms of Queen Elizabeth the Queen Mother, which appear in the fly of her standard, consist of a lion within a double tressure (similar to the Royal Arms of Scotland except that the design is blue on a silver field) quartered with three long-bows *proper* (a heraldic term meaning in their natural colour) on an ermine field (white with black markings). This is a splendid example of heraldic punning, for the Queen Mother's family name is Bowes-Lyon.

As Princess Elizabeth, the Queen flew the Royal Standard, *differenced*, as the heralds say, by the white label with three points which forms the recognized emblem of a child of a king (the label of a king's grandchild has five points). On the centre point of the label was the Tudor Rose; on each of its two outer points was the St. George's Cross.

The Standard of Charles, Prince of Wales, consists of the Royal Standard differenced by the usual three-pointed label: it bears at its centre a shield on which appear the arms of Wales; above the shield is a Prince's Crown (Plate II, figure 8).

The label of the Princess Anne places a red heart on its central point

Standard of Queen Elizabeth the Queen Mother

and a red St. George's Cross on the two other points. That of the Princess Margaret bears a thistle on its centre point and a Tudor Rose on each of the two outer points. That of the Duke of Gloucester has a red lion in the centre point and a red St. George's Cross on the two outer points. The

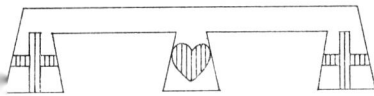

Princess Anne

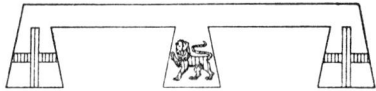

Duke of Gloucester

Princess Margaret

Duke of Kent

five-pointed label of the Duke of Kent—a grandson of King George V— bears a blue anchor on three of the points, a red cross on the other two.

These labels appear on the Royal Standard. Other members of the Royal

Standard of the
Principality of Wales

Family fly the Standard without a label, but surrounded with an ermine border—white with a black marking in each corner, two others along the top and bottom, and one on each side.

The Standard of the Principality of Wales displays four lions, red on gold in the first and fourth quarters and gold on red in the second and third. These arms are centuries old and were borne by such Princes of North Wales as Llewellyn ap Griffith and Owain Glyndwr. The Personal Flag used by Prince Charles during his visits to Wales places at their centre the special coronet of the Prince of Wales approved by King Charles II (see page xii).

3

NATIONAL FLAGS OF THE BRITISH ISLES

What is the flag of England? Winds of the world, declare!

RUDYARD KIPLING: THE FLAG OF ENGLAND

IT may seem strange that war flags should bear a cross, the Christian emblem and sign of peace. Yet throughout history peace-loving men have had to fight in self-defence and to protect their ideals from savage enemies who aimed at destroying them. Frequently we ourselves have had to do so.

Our forefathers felt no hesitation about putting the cross on their battle-flags. They did this not so much because it formed an effective design as because it was the Christian emblem. They aimed at making their flags symbolize the ideals for which they fought.

The Emperor Constantine, who in the fourth century ruled over the greater part of Europe, is said to have had a vision in which he saw in the sky a cross, bearing the words, 'In this sign conquer'. He made the cross the sign of his army and in that sign he did conquer; and he established Christianity as the religion of his empire.

There is a legend that the Crusaders in the Holy Land similarly had a vision of St. George coming to their aid with an army of 'heavenly warriors'. They therefore made his cross their emblem, the blood-red cross on the white background; and three countries chose him as their patron saint. One of these was England.

Little is known about St. George, except that his cross presumably shows that he suffered martyrdom for the Christian faith. He is said to have slain a dragon: this may mean that he actually slaughtered some dangerous monster, a crocodile maybe or a huge snake, but it is more probably a poetic way of honouring his stand against the forces of heathendom, as fierce as any ravening beast.

Whatever his deeds may have been, St. George has long been regarded as one of the greatest of warrior saints. During the Middle Ages his cross was placed on the soldiers' uniforms and flags, and was carried into battle with their armies (Plate III, figure 1). The English used his name as a battle-cry, 'God for Harry, England, and St. George'. His day was, and indeed still is, celebrated on April 23rd. It seemed appropriate that this anniversary should be the date of one of the most heroic deeds of the 1914–18 War, the blocking of Zeebrugge.

The St. George's Cross, red on white, both formed a flag in itself, and appeared in the canton of many other flags. Ensigns in which it appeared were used as distinguishing marks of ships and of such regiments as the

13

London Train Bands, the forerunners of our Territorial and Army Volunteer Reserve. It was still the national flag of England when James I came to the throne.

Just as St. George was the patron saint of England, so St. Andrew was that of Scotland. Brother of St. Peter and the first disciple of Christ, he too was martyred for his faith. Some of his remains are said to have been taken to Scotland, to the town of Kilrymont in Fife, which was afterwards known as St. Andrews. He was later adopted as the patron saint of Scotland, his day being celebrated on November 30th.

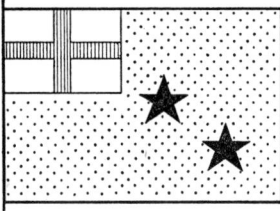

St. Andrew is supposed to have chosen to be crucified on a cross made of two diagonal beams, because he considered himself unworthy to suffer the same death

Typical Flag of London
Train Bands

as that of Christ on an upright cross. A cross of this type—or as the heralds call it, a *saltire*—white on a blue field, therefore became his emblem (Plate III, figure 2).

The Scots placed his saltire on their flag, and on the uniforms of their armies. During the fighting which for centuries ravaged the Scottish Border, the two crosses, so very different both in colour and in form, must have been almost a perfect method of distinguishing friend from foe. And probably if any member of the warring armies had been asked whether the two crosses could ever be united, he would have declared it as impossible as that Englishmen and Scotsmen could live together in peace.

When King James VI of Scotland also became King James I of England, he gave his heralds the very difficult task of combining the two crosses to form one flag. The heralds found it impossible to combine them so as to make them exactly equal: the best they could do was to place the St. George's Cross on a field formed by the St. Andrew's flag. They also gave it the usual fimbriation, by edging it with the metal white, so that the two colours red and blue should not touch. This *First Union Flag* appeared in 1606.

Neither the English nor the Scots welcomed the new flag, which must have at first seemed strange and unnatural. The English protested that the white field of the St. George's Cross was obscured by the St. Andrew's blue. The Scots complained even more bitterly that though the St. George's Cross was left entire it not merely obscured the St. Andrew's Cross but actually cut it into pieces; and they resented this as a slur on their nation. Such protests were of no avail, and the best the nationalists could secure was that the older flags should be flown as well as the new. Ships of both countries—the flag was meant chiefly for use at sea—were to wear the new flag on their mainmasts, the most honourable position: those of South

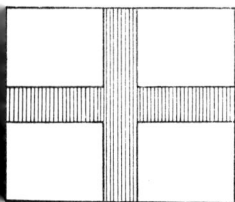

St. George's Cross

St. Andrew's Cross

First Union Flag

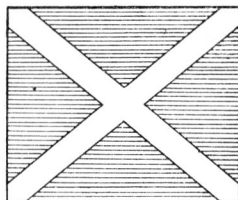

Britain were also to carry the Red Cross on their foremasts, and those of North Britain the White.

In 1634 Charles I reserved the James flag exclusively for the use of royal vessels; merchantmen were to show only a red flag with the St. George's Cross in the canton as an ensign and the St. George's Cross alone as a jack. Later Queen Anne was to reserve it for the Royal Navy, ordering merchantmen, whether English or Scottish, to wear what we should now call a Red Ensign with the James Union in the canton. This custom prevailed until 1801, when the National Flag had again to be altered to symbolize the United Kingdom of Great Britain and Ireland.

The James flag went out of use during the Commonwealth, which produced several flag designs, none of them pleasing in appearance. They were even less satisfactory to the Scots, for when they included the St. Andrew's Cross they gave it the second quarter, whereas the St. George's Cross of England went in the place of honour, the first.

At the time of the Restoration the James flag came back and remained unaltered for many years.

The patron saint of Ireland, St. Patrick, had far more to do with that country than St. George had with England or St. Andrew with Scotland. He was a bishop who, as the leader of a group of missionaries, did much to convert Ireland to Christianity; the Irish people revere his memory, and delight to celebrate his day, March 17th. As, however, he did not suffer martyrdom, he is incorrectly represented by a cross, the martyr's emblem. It is hard to see why the red saltire on a white field, which was the coat of arms of a noble family, should have become known as St. Patrick's Cross.

This red saltire was the emblem now chosen to represent Ireland on the Union Flag. To place its arms down the centre of those of the St. Andrew's Cross would be to destroy this completely and to embitter the Scots still further. The heralds therefore made its red arms run alongside the white arms of the St. Andrew's Cross, with, of course, the usual fimbriation on its other side to prevent the red from touching the blue. They also moved both crosses a little aside, so that the dividing line ran exactly to

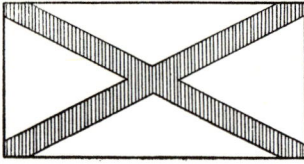

St. Patrick's Cross

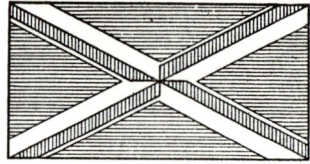

Its Arms Counterchanged

the corner and they *counterchanged* them, an arrangement easier to illustrate than to describe in words.

This was the origin of our present Union Flag (Frontispiece, figure 2), which in heraldic language is thus described:

Azure, the Crosses Saltire of St. Andrew and St. Patrick Quarterly, per Saltire counterchanged *argent* and *gules*: the latter fimbriated of the second, surmounted by the Cross of St. George of the third, fimbriated as the Saltire.

Here *the latter* means St. Patrick's Cross; *of the second* and *of the third* mean the second and third colours mentioned, white and red. It must be admitted that 'heraldic' is not always as easy to understand as one would wish.

This arrangement of the two saltires means that the Union Flag is not quite symmetrical: one half is not an exact mirror-image of the other. Thus we have two different ways of flying it, one correct and the other quite wrong.

The Union Flag is flown correctly when the Cross of St. Andrew is *above* that of St. Patrick *in the hoist* (as the earlier of the two to be placed on the flag it is entitled to the more honourable position) and *below* it *in the fly.* In simple language: at the end next the pole the broad white stripe goes on top.

Unfortunately many people either do not know this or do not trouble to act on it. Whenever flags are used as decorations a number of them are flown upside-down, with the St. Patrick's Cross above the St. Andrew's in the hoist (i.e. the red stripe on top next the pole). This is sometimes described as a signal of distress, like any other flag flown upside-down, but it is doubtful whether it is so used: from a distance or in bad weather it would be hard to distinguish whether the Union Flag were correctly flown or not.

Although it is clear how the Union Flag is to be flown, however, it is not so clear who is entitled to fly it. The older heraldic view is that it is properly a royal flag and indeed a coat of arms; in the form of a shield and ensigned by the Royal Crown, it is one of the Royal Badges. When the present design was made official in 1801 it was ordered to be flown on all His Majesty's forts, castles, etc.—and not by His Majesty's subjects.

Thus it might be argued that it should be flown over Windsor Castle except when the Queen is in residence, but not over Buckingham Palace, for that is not a fort. It is, moreover, hoisted over Government buildings— offices and national museums and picture-galleries—on official days of rejoicing (see Appendix 1). On this view it is an emblem of 'Her Majesty's Service', and should not be used by ordinary citizens: their flag is either, on land as on sea, the Red Ensign, or the St. George's or St. Andrew's Cross.

Nevertheless most of us do fly the Union Flag. We think of it as our flag, and we should feel very aggrieved if we were forbidden to use it. Its use is a long-established custom which fortunately is never likely to be interfered with. It was, indeed, announced in Parliament some years ago that because the Union is the national flag, every member of the nation is entitled to fly it on land. Whether or not the heralds would agree with this announcement, one thing is perfectly clear: whenever the Union Flag is flown it certainly ought to be flown the right way up.

As we all know, the national flag is generally called the Union Jack— a name which dates at least from the reign of Queen Anne—but the reason for this is uncertain. Several attempts have been made to discover its origin. It may come from the 'jack-et' of the English or Scottish soldiers; or from the name of King James I who originated the first Union, in either its Latin or French form, Jacobus or Jacques; or, as 'jack' once meant small, the name may come from a proclamation issued by Charles II that the Union Flag should be flown only by ships of the Royal Navy as a *jack*, a small flag at the bowsprit. (This jack was hoisted on a *staff* on the bowsprit or stem of a ship.) Though there is no definite proof, this last explanation seems the most probable.

The smaller islands of Great Britain have their own national flags. The device of the Isle of Man consists of three white and yellow legs united at the thigh, and is flown on a red field (Plate III, figure 6). This *Trinacria*, as it is called, is based on an ancient emblem of Sicily; it also appears in the fly of the Red Ensign.

There is a saying that the Channel Islands do not 'belong' to England —that England on the other hand 'belongs' to the Channel Islands! (They form the last remaining portions of the Dukedom of Normandy, whose ruler, William, conquered England in 1066.) The Lieutenant-Governors of the larger islands fly the Union Flag, with special emblems at its centre. That of Jersey consists of a red shield bearing three gold leopards (or lions) differing slightly from those on the Royal Standard; this was the badge of Richard the Lion-heart (another King of England who was also Duke of Normandy). Guernsey uses the same device, but with a sprig of gold leaves above the shield. Alderney has a green circle with a gold border; on it is a golden lion, something like the Scottish lion but with a red crown, tongue and claws and holding in its paw a sprig of green leaves (Plate III, figures 7, 9, and 8). The shield of Alderney appears in its local flag at the centre of a St. George's Cross. The flag of Sark places two gold lions in the red canton of a St. George's Cross, half of the lower of the two lions being in the arm of the Cross.

The St. Patrick's Saltire, red on white, is also flown in Jersey and the St. George's Cross in Guernsey—but on land only, for as a flag of the Royal Navy it cannot be flown at sea except to indicate the presence of an Admiral.

Nothing representing Wales appears on either the Royal Standard or the Union Flag; the Principality is no doubt included in England, as it often is in everyday speech. Welshmen can console themselves for this omission, however, by reflecting that their own emblem is the oldest in the country. The Red Cross of St. George dates only from the Crusades; the Lions on the Royal Standard may have 'come over with William the Conqueror', but the Dragon of the Welsh flag had been here a thousand years when the Conqueror came.

The Dragon emblem is very old indeed; it is full of strange magical meaning which students of early history are trying to understand. The Romans who invaded Britain brought it from the east, and it remained in two different forms after they had gone. The Golden Dragon became the symbol of Wessex, and later of all England; the English used it as a banner during the Danish invasions, and it floated over Harold's forces at the Battle of Hastings.

Y Ddraig Goch, the Red Dragon with extended wings, became the flag of Wales, and is flown by Welshmen on days of rejoicing and especially on St. David's Day, March 1st. The flag had two slightly different designs: in that usually flown, the field is half-green and half-white (Plate III, figure 5). Another version consists of a flag with a white field, the green appearing only beneath the dragon's feet. The colours of the field, white and green, were those of the Tudors, and the flag resembles that flown by Henry Tudor, Earl of Richmond, at the Battle of Bosworth, by which he became King Henry VII.

Badge of Wales

In 1953 Queen Elizabeth II decided that the Red Dragon should be 'honourably augmented' by enclosure in a scroll surmounted by the Royal Crown. The motto on the scroll is taken from an ancient Welsh poem and means 'The Red Dragon lends impetus'. The badge is placed at the centre of the flag, which is divided horizontally, white above green. The older flag, however, may still be used.

FLAGS AND BADGES OF THE BRITISH ISLES

1. England (St. George's Cross)

2. Scotland (St. Andrew's Cross)

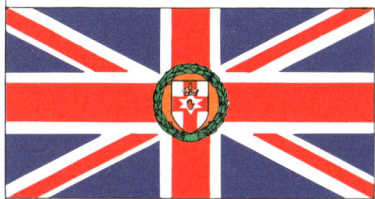

3. Northern Ireland (Governor's Flag)

4. Irish Republic (Eire)

5. Wales (Red Dragon)

6. Isle of Man

7. Jersey

8. Alderney

9. Guernsey

Plate III

The development of the modern Union Flag did not completely replace the older flags. The earlier form of the Union, the James flag without the St. Patrick's Cross, still appears in one modern ensign. This is flown by the Commissioners of Northern Lighthouses, who are responsible for all lighthouses and lightships off the coast of Scotland. Their flag is unique in being a white ensign, *without* a St. George's Cross like that of the Navy; it shows a lighthouse in its fly; and it has the old Union Flag in the canton. The Blue Ensign flown by the Scottish lighthouses and their store-depots and tenders is, however, of modern type, and the lighthouse displayed in its fly is white.

Commissioners of
Northern Lighthouses

For over fifty years Ireland has been divided, but in neither of its two divisions is the St. Patrick's Cross much flown. The people of Northern Ireland proclaim that they are still part of the United Kingdom and of the British Commonwealth by flying the same Union Flag that we fly in Great Britain (Frontispiece, figure 2).

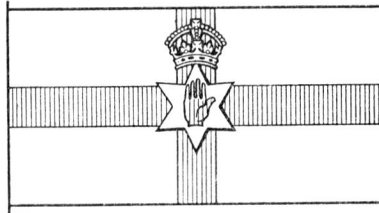

In 1953 Northern Ireland was granted a new flag: at the centre of the St. George's Cross the Royal Crown surmounts a six-pointed star bearing the traditional 'Red Hand of Ulster'.

Northern Ireland

The people in the southern part of Ireland, Eire, show that their country is a sovereign independent democratic state by flying their own national flag, a tricolour of green, white, and orange. The colour is definitely not yellow as is sometimes shown: it is a warm orange-gold, described by the heralds as *tenné* (Plate III, figure 4).

This flag is said to be over a hundred years old, and to have been suggested by the French tricolour, though it makes use of the traditional Irish colours. The national colour of the 'Emerald Isle' is, of course, green, and this was adopted by the Irish Nationalist organizations and so by Eire. The colour of Northern Ireland comes from the title of that English King whom its people still delight to honour, William of Orange. The central white signifies peace and unity between the people of Northern Ireland and of Eire, between Orange and Green.

This tricolour forms not only the National Flag of Eire, but also the Merchant Flag and the Ensign. The Jack displays a golden harp on a green field; the President's Flag places it on a blue field.

It has been said that, to make it symbolize the whole Commonwealth, some emblem ought to be added to the Union Flag representing 'Britain beyond the seas'. No such alteration is likely to be made. The flag which represented 'Greater Britain' throughout two world wars may well continue to do so in peace.

4

FLAGS OF THE ROYAL NAVY

Whose flag has braved a thousand years
The battle and the breeze.

THOMAS CAMPBELL: YE MARINERS OF ENGLAND

A GREAT English writer, whose enthusiasm for world peace made him cold towards such national emblems as uniforms and flags, poked fun at these lines by saying that it was a strange thing to happen to a flag which was hardly a hundred years old.

He, of course, meant the present Union Flag, but the poet Campbell clearly meant nothing of the kind. His verses no more refer to one special design than they do to one special piece of bunting: they speak of the various flags which the Royal Navy has flown during its history—a history which has lasted considerably more than a thousand years.

The earliest English flag, on sea as well as on land, may have been the Golden Dragon of Wessex, under which the English forces warred against the Danes. The earliest sea-flags of which we have definite record date from the thirteenth century: they are mostly Saints' emblems and royal or noble coats of arms like those used on land. By the sixteenth century one flag had come into use by all English ships, men-of-war and merchantmen alike: it bore the emblem which still appears on the Royal Navy's flag today, the St. George's Cross.

This cross not only formed a flag in itself; it also appeared in the cantons of a surprising number of ensigns. Some of these resembled those of our own time, having their field coloured red, white, or blue. Others consisted of variously coloured stripes, slanting in the time of Queen Elizabeth I, horizontal in that of the Stuarts. A pattern of narrow stripes is not usually attractive, and to this rule only one of these ensigns, that of the East India Company, formed an exception; more striking than the others, it was to have a great future.

When James I introduced the first British flag, this did not completely displace the older flags. Some English ships wore the St. George's Cross and some Scottish ships the St. Andrew's; others preferred ensigns with the appropriate cross in the canton. Similarly, some ships of the Royal Navy wore the new British flag. The emblem combining the two crosses did not, however, appear in the canton of the ensigns until 1707.

The Royal Navy discontinued the use of the striped ensigns, and carried only those whose fields consisted of one of the three national colours. These served two purposes: they distinguished the various squadrons of a battle-fleet, and also indicated the seniority of its commanders. Perhaps because the red ensign was the oldest of the three, an Admiral of the Red ranked above an Admiral of the White, who in turn was superior to an Admiral of the Blue.

This arrangement, however, proved clumsy and confusing. Nelson at Trafalgar realized that the red and blue ensigns might be mistaken for the enemy's flags; himself a Vice-Admiral of the White, he ordered all his ships to wear the White Ensign. In 1864 this became the distinctive flag of the Royal Navy: it is not an ensign with a plain white field, but a St. George's Cross with the Union in the canton (Plate IV, figure 1).

The White Ensign is essentially the flag of the Royal Navy, and no merchant ship is permitted to fly it. There is a heavy fine for its misuse, and if wrongly flown it may be confiscated, if necessary by force. The Royal Yacht Squadron, however, hold a warrant to fly it.

Ashore, it is flown over some Naval Establishments. These generally bear such names as H.M.S. *Drake* (the Royal Naval Barracks at Plymouth). In the Navy they are often referred to as 'Stone Frigates'—permanently anchored and unable to put to sea!

A few churches sometimes fly the White Ensign. Many retired officers of the Royal Navy delight to fly the flag under which they served, and although this is not officially authorized, nobody is likely to grudge them its use. It is quite clear, however, that the White Ensign is a flag which no landsman ought to fly on shore.

H.M. Ships and Naval Establishments hoist the White Ensign in the morning at an hour varying with the season and lower it at sunset, its hoisting and lowering being carried out ceremonially. While it is being hoisted work stops, a guard is mounted, and all officers and men on deck face the Colours and salute or stand to attention. The band plays the National Anthem as the flag is slowly hoisted, the last notes sounding as it reaches the truck; if there is no band the *Salute* is sounded on the bugle. (At sea the Colours are frequently flown day and night.) When the Flag is lowered the bugle sounds *Sunset*.

The White Ensign is dipped as a sign of courtesy when a ship of the Royal Navy meets a foreign vessel—but only on condition that the 'foreigner' first dips his own flag.

The Executive Branch of the Royal Navy has as its duty the actual command and handling of the ships. An officer of this branch above the rank of captain is called a Flag-Officer because, when he is in command, the ship which carries him wears a special flag. The officer who at one time was responsible for the Royal Navy was the Lord High Admiral, and he—after he ceased to fly the Royal Standard as representing the Sovereign—flew his own emblem of command, the Admiralty Flag. The last Lord High Admiral to fly this flag at sea (in 1827) was the Duke of Clarence, who afterwards became King William IV.

This post was for some time abolished, and its duties performed by the Lords Commissioners of the Admiralty; they included not only the Sea Lords, senior Naval Officers of wide experience, but civilians with special knowledge, headed by a Cabinet Minister. They accordingly flew the Admiralty Flag, a gold anchor and cable on a red field.

In 1964, however, when the Admiralty became part of the newly formed Ministry of Defence, Queen Elizabeth II resumed the title of Lord High Admiral. The Admiralty Flag is therefore worn, like the Royal Standard, over

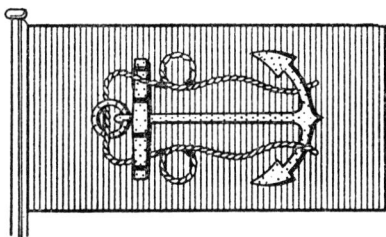

Admiralty Flag

any ship in which the Queen embarks—for she is the supreme head of the Royal Navy. It is not dipped in salute, nor is it usually half-masted as a token of mourning; only on the death of the Sovereign is it lowered to half-mast.

As Lord High Admiral of the United Kingdom, the Queen thus flies the Admiralty Flag, and she also flies the Union Flag. The Royal Yacht *Britannia*, when the Queen is aboard, wears the Royal Standard at the main mast-head, the Admiralty Flag at the fore, the Union Flag at the mizzen, and the White Ensign and Union Jack on their respective staffs.

An Admiral of the Fleet—the highest naval rank—flies, when afloat, the national emblem of Britain, the Union Flag. An Admiral of the Executive Branch flies the older national emblem of England, the St. George's Cross. A Vice-Admiral flies a similar Cross, but with one red ball (circle) in the canton; a Rear-Admiral has a second ball in the lower part of the hoist. (On the coloured ensigns formerly flown by Admirals of the Red and of the Blue, these ranks were indicated by *white* balls.)

A Commodore flies a Broad Pendant, a flag also bearing the St. George's

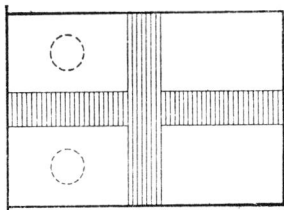

Admiral's Flag

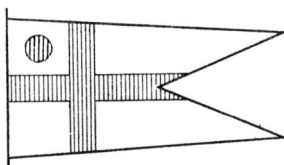

Commodore's Broad Pendant

Cross but tapering slightly and ending in a swallow-tail, and with a red ball in the canton. A Commodore on the Active List of the Royal Naval

Reserve flies a similar Pendant, except that the cross is not red but blue, and there is no ball in the canton. When two or more Navy ships lie in the same port, the senior officer flies a Broad Pendant like that of a Commodore but smaller.

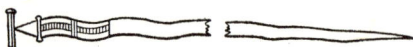

Commission Pendant

Unless a Flag-Officer is on board, an officer below the rank of Commodore who commands a ship flies the Commission Pendant. This is white, with the St. George's Cross in the hoist. In the days when the Royal Navy had many large ships it might be as long as twenty feet; nowadays, however, it is normally nine feet long. From a breadth of several inches at the hoist it tapers to an inch and a half. The Paying-off Pendant, flown as a sign of rejoicing when a ship is returning home at the end of her commission, is even longer and tapers even more gently—it may indeed be so long that its point has to be supported by a bladder floating on the sea! (Its length is usually the same as that of the ship, but is increased in the case of longer commissions.) This Pendant is not an 'official issue', but is made from any bunting which the Signalmen can 'scrounge'; its name comes from the old days when crews were engaged for each cruise and paid off at its end.

The practice of flying the Commission Pendant may date from our wars with Holland, at one time a mighty sea-power.

The Church Pendant, flown during Divine Service, may also date from these wars, for it bears the Red Cross of England in the hoist and the red, white, and blue of the Netherlands in the fly.

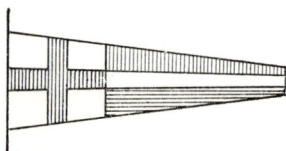

Church Pendant

In addition to the White Ensign on the ensign staff, ships of the Royal Navy also wear a Union Flag on the jackstaff. Flown at the peak this is a sign that a court martial is sitting. During the First World War there was found to be a risk of confusing the White Ensign with the old German Imperial Naval Flag, which also had a white field. The Royal Navy therefore carried a second battle flag as well as the White Ensign; this for a time was the Red Ensign (for a few days it was the Blue Ensign) but for the greater part of the War it was the Union Flag. Each ship wore several White Ensigns, so that if one were destroyed by the enemy's fire it would not be mistaken for a sign of surrender.

After that war, King George V approved a King's Colour for the Royal Navy, to be carried by formal Guards of Honour when parading ashore. It is a silk flag, resembling the Queen's Colour of an infantry regiment, but consists not of the Union Flag but of the White Ensign. At its centre an heraldic Garter encloses a red circle on which is the Royal Crown and

Cypher, E.R. At less formal parades abroad, naval parties sometimes carry the White Ensign similar to that flown by their ships.

The Blue Ensign of the Royal Naval Auxiliary Service bears in the fly a badge representing a mine floating on the waves and encircled by a cable above which is a Naval Crown (Plate IV, figure 4).

The flag of the Sea Cadet Corps is a Blue Ensign, bearing the Corps badge in white: the Anchor and Cable surrounded by a double circle which bears the title of the Corps; above is the Naval Crown, in which two sails separate the stems of three eighteenth-century ships, and below is the Corps motto 'Ready Aye Ready'.

The Royal Marines, like regiments of infantry, have both a Queen's and a Regimental Colour; these consist respectively of the Union Flag and the Blue Ensign. The design on each of their Colours includes an Anchor, the Royal Crown and Cypher, the word 'Gibraltar' and the Royal Marines' badge, a globe surrounded by a laurel wreath, and motto *Per Mare per Terram* ('By Sea, by Land').

Sea Cadet Corps

The use of flags to convey orders and information must be very old: hand-signals could be made easier to recognize by waving some conspicuous

A Queen's Colour of the Royal Navy

A Regimental Colour of the Royal Marines

object such as a flag. More elaborate methods were also used: Sir Walter Raleigh devised a form of signalling by striking and at once re-hoisting one or other of the sails.

As early as the fourteenth century the Royal Navy made flag-signals. A flag half-way up the mast called the captains into council; hoisted to the mast-head it gave the warning 'Enemy in sight'. By the seventeenth century, flags, including the ordinary national emblems, conveyed meanings by the positions in which they were flown.

The first definite flag code was compiled in the eighteenth century. Each represented a number, 1 to 9, and 0; there were also a 'preparative' flag, flags meaning 'yes' and 'no', and a 'substitute' flag. By using these flags singly or in twos and threes, a large number of different 'hoists' could be made, each with a meaning which was explained in the code-book. The 'substitute' was used to avoid the necessity for duplicate flags, when the same flag number occurred twice in one hoist.

Some colours appeared blurred when seen from a distance: whatever its pattern, a flag coloured red and blue simply looked like purple. The easiest flags to recognize were those coloured yellow and blue, or white and red or black or blue. The designs of the flags were changed several times in an attempt to make them unmistakable.

Such a ten-flag code enabled Nelson to give his famous signal at Trafalgar. The flags he used are illustrated below, and the signal ran: 253 (England) 269 (expects) 863 (that) 261 (every) 471 (man) 958 (will) 220—or rather 2 'substitute' 0—(do) 370 (his) 4 (d) 21 (u) 19 (t) 24 (y). The word 'duty'

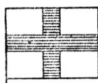
1

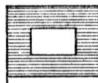
2

3

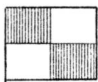
4

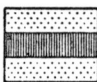
5

6

7

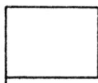
8

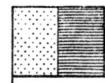
9

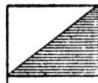
0

Substitute

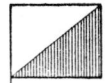
Telegraph

THE SIGNAL CODE USED BY NELSON AT TRAFALGAR

had to be spelled because it did not appear in the code-book. (These flags are flown every year on Trafalgar Day, 21 October, by H.M.S. *Victory* at Portsmouth, and from the base of the Nelson Column in Trafalgar Square on the nearest Sunday to Trafalgar Day.) A special 'Telegraph' Flag was also flown to show which code was being used, and Nelson's signal was at once followed by another, which flew until it was shot away: 16, 'Engage the enemy more closely'.

The method of signalling now used by the Royal Navy is much more complicated. For communicating with merchant ships it uses the International Code of Signals, described in a later chapter. For its own use it employs the flags and pendants of the International Code, with the addition of ten Numerical Flags, nine Special Flags, ten Special Pendants, and a fourth 'Substitute' Flag. The meaning of the various hoists is, of course, kept secret and is changed from time to time; at one time the code-book used to be weighted and had to be at once thrown into the sea if in danger of capture.

FLAGS OF THE BRITISH ARMY

A moth-eaten rag on a worm-eaten pole—
It does not seem likely to stir a man's soul.
'Tis the deeds that were done 'neath that moth-eaten rag
When the pole was a staff and the rag was a flag.

SIR EDWARD HAMLEY: THE OLD COLOURS OF THE FORTY-THIRD

UNLIKE the Royal Navy and the Royal Air Force, the British Army had no special flag until in 1938 King George VI gave his approval to an Army flag. It consists of the Royal Crest, a crowned lion standing on a Royal Crown, placed at the junction of two crossed swords, on a red field (Plate IV, figure 2).

Again unlike those of the Royal Navy, each of the different units of the Cavalry and Infantry has its own special ceremonial flags, called its Colours. In the old days of hand-to-hand fighting and short-range weapons, these emblems were taken into action, and served the same purpose as the Admirals' Flags and Commodores' Pendants, to mark the presence of high-ranking officers. Their designs were, however, not standardized but were based on the different coats of arms of the officers who commanded the various Units.

These leaders' flags naturally served as rallying-points round which the struggle raged fiercest. Naturally, too, they became trophies which men would gladly die to capture or to defend. The Colours aroused deep feelings of patriotism, loyalty, and pride; they gained almost a religious meaning. It seemed quite proper that their tattered remnants should be hung on the walls of places of worship.

As the range of modern weapons lengthened, the Colours became useless as rallying-points; indeed, they were needlessly dangerous to those who carried them or rallied round them. The Colours were, therefore, no longer taken into battle but were left instead in the custody of the regimental headquarters. They were last officially carried into action at the battle of Laing's Nek, in the First Boer War, on January 28th, 1883, but at least one Regiment took its Colours, quite unofficially, into the Front Line in France during the First World War. Today they would be as much out of place in the long-range bombardments and tank battles of mechanized warfare—to say nothing of nuclear weapons—as they would be in the 'unarmed combat' of the Commandos.

The Regimental Colours are nowadays used only for ceremonial purposes, to add to the dignity of inspections, guards of honour, and reviews, and are

FLAGS OF THE SERVICES

1. Royal Navy (White Ensign)

2. Army

3. Royal Air Force

4. Royal Naval Auxiliary Service

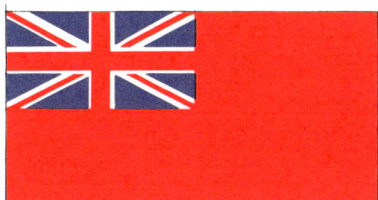

5. Merchant Navy (Red Ensign)

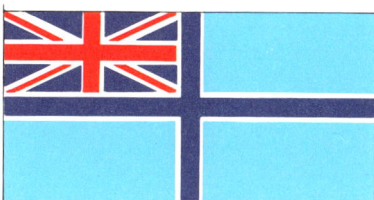

6. Civil Air Service

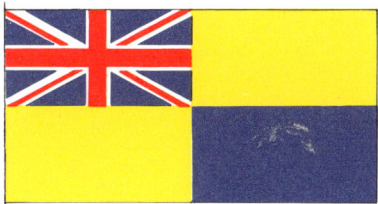

7. Civil Defence

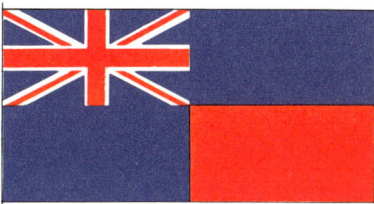

8. National Fire Service
(obsolete)

Plate IV

seldom uncased except at such parades. Even then the officer who carries them holds them in his hand and allows them to fly only during the actual salute. If royalty be present, they are lowered to the ground.

When a member of the Royal Family presents new Colours to a regiment, the officer receiving them kneels on one knee. The Colours are then con-

Standard of the Blues and
Royals

Regimental Colour
of the Welsh Guards

secrated by the regimental chaplain: as of old, it is not thought that defence of one's people is inconsistent with Christianity. Trooping the Colour is an impressive ceremony during which it is borne along the ranks to the accompaniment of stirring music; it is held on such national anniversaries as the Queen's Birthday. Old Colours which go out of service when new Colours are presented are similarly trooped before being taken to their last resting-place on the walls of cathedral or church.

Regimental Colours are made of silk and bear an elaborately embroidered design. They are fringed with gold except on one side; this consists of a broad hem, through which passes the Colour Pike, surmounted by a gilt Royal Crest. The Colours are pierced with an eyeletted hole, through which passes a gold cord, ending in tassels, that fastens them to two rings on the pike.

The Household Cavalry and the Dragoon Guards carry rectangular Standards; other Cavalry Regiments carry Guidons, with their flies divided and rounded; the name comes from the French words *guide-homme*, meaning, 'a guide to the men'. The Household Cavalry has banners suspended from the state trumpet and swathed round their drums. The Royal Artillery do not carry Colours, for their symbol consists of their guns; nor do the various corps whose purpose is not so much to fight as to serve the fighting-men. The Royal Artillery, however, has its Standards flown at the Headquarters of the various Units: a pendant, rounded in the fly, and displaying three old-fashioned cannon, the Crown, and the Artillery watchword *Ubique* ('Everywhere').

Infantry Battalions, other than those of Rifle Regiments, each carry two Colours, the Queen's and the Regimental; both are embroidered with the names of the battles in which the regiment distinguished itself. In the Foot Guards, the Queen's Colour is scarlet, the Regimental Colour is a Union Flag. In the Line Regiments, on the other hand, the Queen's Colour consists of the Union Flag, its centre bearing the name of the Regiment and the Royal Crown. The Regimental Colour is a flag of one colour, that of the regiment's facings: except that if these be white it bears a broad St. George's Cross. On both Colours appear the battle honours of the regiment. Small flags, bearing emblems similar to those on the Colours, are sometimes used to mark out the saluting base on ceremonial parades.

A modern battlefield is no place for Colours. Still, however, there is as great a need as ever to mark the whereabouts in the field of the various commanders.

For this purpose flags are still used. They fly over the tents or buildings where commanding officers make their headquarters; and similar flags, though much smaller, are carried on their staff cars. They also flutter over the ungainly shapes of tanks. Such flags are, however, very different from the ceremonial Colours. With few exceptions they have no heraldic meaning. Both in material (not silk but bunting) and in design they are, as people say nowadays, functional. They are simply directing signs, as lamps are by night, to the headquarters which they indicate, and they arouse no patriotic feelings. No fierce struggles are waged to secure or defend them, and if a similar flag were captured from an enemy it would only be a matter of interest to Intelligence.

Until it was merged with the Defence Council in 1964, the Army Council—the committee of high-ranking officers and civilian organizers headed by a Cabinet Minister which formerly controlled the Army—had its own flag, the Union, charged in its centre by a shield bearing the arms of the old Board of Ordnance: three old-fashioned cannon arranged one above

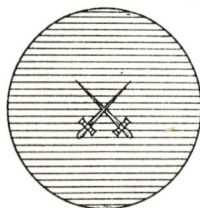

Royal Corps
of Transport

the other, gold on a blue field; above them are three old-fashioned cannonballs, side by side, white, but shaded so as to appear round, on a white field.

Military Authorities—Army Officers of high rank—have special flags to be hoisted over the ships on which they embark. That flown by a General Officer Commanding is the Union Flag with the Royal Crown and Cypher at its centre (gold and red on blue). The flag used by the Royal Corps of Transport is the Blue Ensign with crossed swords (gold, red, and white) in its fly. In 1967 a similar Ensign was approved by Queen Elizabeth II for use by Army vessels.

The flag of the Women's Royal Army Corps is divided horizontally beech brown (reddish-brown) and green and displays at its centre the Corps badge: a white lioness (shaded grey) within a gold wreath surmounted by the Royal Crown.

Women's Royal Army Corps

6

FLAGS OF THE ROYAL AIR FORCE
AND THE CIVIL AIR SERVICE

Per ardua ad astra. ('Through Hardship to the Stars')

THE MOTTO OF THE R.A.F.

AVIATION produced many new flags, though, needless to say, they are not flown on aircraft when these are actually flying. (R.A.F. aircraft are therefore distinguished not by flags but by the well-known red, white, and blue roundel; and British civil aircraft by a group of four letters preceded by the letter 'G'.) They are flown over buildings and airfields; and some of them are also flown in miniature on motor vehicles or from small flagstaffs on aircraft when these are grounded.

The flag of the Royal Air Force is a blue ensign, with the Union Flag in the canton. Its colour is, however, not the dark blue of *the* Blue Ensign but a very light blue, suggesting the hue of the sky. In the fly is the emblem similar to that which appears on the R.A.F. aircraft, the roundel (concentric circles) of red, white, and dark blue (Plate IV, figure 3).

Commanding Officers are entitled to fly distinguishing flags. The designs of these are varying arrangements of the three R.A.F. colours, red, dark blue, and light blue. The flag of Service members of the Air Force Board is a Royal Crown on a background of light blue and dark blue halves.

When the Queen or any other member of the Royal Family is travelling by air, a small Royal or Personal Standard is flown whilst the aircraft is on the ground. Some officers holding very senior appointments fly their individual distinguishing flags and a small R.A.F. Ensign is flown by high officials such as heads of foreign states, Governors General of Commonwealth countries, the Prime Minister and Cabinet Ministers.

The first Colour presented to the Royal Air Force was that presented to the R.A.F. College by King George VI in 1948. Colours have also been presented to the R.A.F. in the United Kingdom, the Near East Air Force, R.A.F. Germany, the R.A.F. Regiment, Cranwell College, the No. 1 School of Technical Training, and the Central Flying School. These are square flags woven in R.A.F. blue silk, fringed in blue and silver, bearing the Royal Cypher. A portion of the Unit Badge features in most Colours and some also have the Union Flag embroidered in the canton. Squadron Standards, which are the equivalent of Regimental Colours, are awarded to operational squadrons. These are also of R.A.F. blue with a border of roses, thistles, shamrocks, and leeks. The Squadron Badge is in the centre and battle honours are inscribed on white scrolls.

The Ocean Weather Ships, owned by the Ministry of Defence and administered by the Meteorological Office, being manned by Merchant Navy crews,

Queen's Colour of the Royal
Air Force in the United
Kingdom

Colour of Cranwell College

at first wore the Red Ensign. In 1948, however, the Admiralty authorized them to wear the Blue Ensign defaced by the appropriate badge. This is in gold and consists of the sun rising over the sea, encircled by the words 'Ocean Weather Ship'; over all is the R.A.F. Eagle.

The Ensign of the Royal Observer Corps is similar to that of the R.A.F., but instead of the roundel it bears the R.O.C. Badge and Motto. This shows an Elizabethan coast-watcher in gold standing on a green verge and holding up a torch; it is surrounded by gold laurels with red berries; above is the Royal Crown and below is a scroll containing the Corps motto, 'Forewarned is Forearmed'.

The Ensign of the Air Training Corps is also light blue, with the Union Flag in the canton and the Corps Badge in the fly: a rising golden falcon within a red, gold-bordered circle bearing the words 'Air Training Corps' in

Badge of Royal
Observer Corps

Badge of the Air
Training Corps

Badge of
Ocean Weather Ships

gold with an Astral Crown above and the Corps motto below: 'Venture Adventure' on a gold scroll.

Simple flags and other symbols are flown on the masts at airfields to give information to pilots.

The Civil Air Ensign, used by commercial and private air transport services, has a light blue field and bears the Union Flag in the canton. It is, however, distinguished not by the R.A.F. Roundel but by a cross of St. George type in dark blue fimbriated with white (Plate IV, figure 6). Aircraft employed in carrying mail bear on their fuselage the words 'Royal Air Mail' in white and a yellow emblem of the Crown and Post-horn.

Commercial aircraft, when grounded in Britain, may fly the Civil Air Ensign; they may also fly the House Flag of the airline to which they belong. When grounded on a foreign airfield, they may fly the British Civil Air Ensign and the flag of the land in which that airfield is situated.

Many airlines have their own House Flags, which may be flown not only on aircraft but over airfields (a large airfield may fly the House Flags of all the airlines which use it) and office buildings, and may even be carried in civic processions. British European Airways, for instance, has a dark green flag bearing an arrow-shaped emblem formed from the Union Jack; British Overseas Airways Corporation uses a blue flag showing a gold 'Speedbird'. In 1973 these merged with several other regional lines into British Airways, but they have not yet decided on a new flag.

The House Flags of some Dominion and foreign airlines are based on the appropriate national emblem. Air Canada uses a red flag bearing the Maple Leaf; the Australian line Qantas, a flying kangaroo. Air France combines with a modified tricolour of blue, white, and red the emblem of Pegasus, the Flying Horse.

The flag of the British Airports Authority bears, on white, four oblique

British Airports
Authority

stripes, two red and two purple. An airfield may fly not only the Civil Air Ensign and the House Flags, but also a local emblem: thus Guernsey Airfield flies the St. George's Cross. The tube which flies over R.A.F. and Civil Airfields is not so much a flag as an aid to navigation. It is called the wind-sock and combines two ancient ideas. Some of England's early Dragon Flags, like some early Chinese flags, were made double, forming bags which the wind would inflate. In the Middle Ages the archers used streamers of cloth to indicate the wind, so that they could allow for this in aiming their arrows. The wind-sock is similarly inflated, and shows the direction and strength of the wind, thus enabling aircraft pilots to allow for this in taking off and landing.

7

FLAGS AND FUNNELS OF THE MERCHANT NAVY

First of the scattered legions, under a shrieking sky,
Dipping between the rollers, the English flag goes by.

RUDYARD KIPLING: THE FLAG OF ENGLAND

THE Red and Blue Ensigns, no longer flown by the Royal Navy, were available for other uses. Though it has now been replaced by the White Ensign, the Blue Ensign became the flag of the Royal Naval Reserve and remained so for years. A few yacht clubs are permitted to fly it without any distinguishing badge.

When 'defaced' by the appropriate badge in its fly, the Blue Ensign is the flag of some of the Governments of regions in the Commonwealth. In home waters it shows that the ship which flies it is in the service of a Government Department. A number of yacht clubs are also allowed to place their badge in its fly: the Royal Welsh Yacht Club, for example, defaces it with the Royal and Welsh emblems, the Crown over the Prince of Wales' feathers.

The Red Ensign became the flag of the Merchant Navy—known also

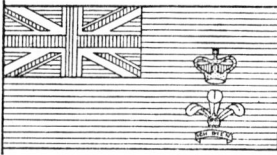

Royal Welsh Yacht Club   Royal Fowey Yacht Club

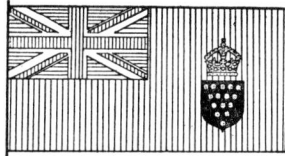

as the Merchant Service. This includes not only merchant ships but all privately owned vessels. When registered in Britain these ships fly the Red Ensign undefaced by any badge; when registered in certain parts of the Commonwealth they fly it defaced by the badge of their own country. Several British yacht clubs are permitted to deface it with their club badge; all others—unless authorized to use the Blue Ensign—fly the Red Ensign undefaced (Plate IV, figure 5).

Whatever its ensign, a yacht club also flies its Club Burgee at the mast-head. A yacht owner may also devise his own personal flag, called his 'House Flag', and a racing yacht flies special racing and prize flags. None of these yachting flags should resemble any national or official emblem.

The Blue and Red Ensigns are usually flown on the ensign staff or gaff.

Ships of the Merchant Navy must hoist them, under penalty of a fine, when ordered to do so by a vessel of the Royal Navy, and when entering or leaving any foreign port, and—except for small craft—any British port. They are forbidden to use any flags resembling those of the Royal Navy or any other national flags.

A vessel requiring a pilot flies the International Code Flag G, striped vertically with three yellow and three blue alternate stripes, the International Code signals UC or UE, or it may fly the Pilot *Jack*, the Union Flag surrounded by a white border, hoisted at the fore. The Pilot *Flag* is flown by the pilot boat and is of large proportions compared with the boat: two horizontal stripes, white above red. This flag should also be flown to indicate that a pilot is on board, although the International Code of Signals requires a vessel to fly 'Flag H', striped vertically white and red, for the same purpose. There is, therefore, an apparent conflict between the use of the Pilot Flag and Flag H; and, although strictly speaking the Pilot Flag should be flown, in fact, as Flag H is bound to be carried by all ships, it is flown more often than the Pilot Flag.

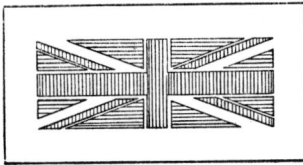

Pilot Jack

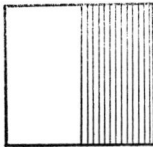

Flag H

While in a foreign port, a merchant ship may fly at the mast-head the merchant flag of the country in which the port is situated; this is intended to show politeness to that country and is called a *Courtesy Flag*.

There is nothing to prevent merchant ships from flying flags plainly different from national emblems. Indeed, many shipping firms, like the airlines, have their own House Flags ('house' is an old word for a business company) to fly over their ships at sea and their offices on land. They may also paint their ships' funnels a distinctive colour, so that with the flags these serve as a combined trade-mark and advertisement, proclaiming the ownership of the different lines. The House Flag is usually worn at the main mast-head, but the firm of Cunard-Brocklebank Ltd. (black funnels with a white-and-blue band) wears its flag at the foremast, white in the hoist and blue in the fly (Plate V, figure 1).

The White Ensign itself, defaced by a badge, was once used as a House Flag. It was flown by the Royal Niger Company, which owned a fleet of steamers, but after a few years was replaced by the Blue Ensign similarly defaced, and later this was withdrawn. The badge, placed across the arm of the St. George's Cross in the fly, was a white red-bordered circle containing a black Y-shaped emblem; the arms of this bore the Latin words *Ars, Jus, Pax* ('Art, Right, Peace').

Some of the hundreds of British House Flags are centuries old and some are heraldic in origin. The oldest and most beautiful of these flags has vanished from the sea, for the Muscovy Company no longer exists. Queen Elizabeth I, in granting it a charter to trade with Russia, allowed it to fly the St. George's Cross, properly fimbriated with a white edging, on a field consisting of the English Arms (Plate V, figure 2).

Queen Elizabeth I also granted to the East India Company a charter to trade with India. Its flag was one of the old striped ensigns; its field consisted of thirteen horizontal stripes, seven red and six white. Its canton at first contained the St. George's Cross and later the King James combined crosses of St. George and St. Andrew. (Plate VIII, figure 2.)

The Hudson's Bay Company (yellow funnels), whose charter to trade with the North American tribes was granted by Charles II, was the only firm allowed to use the Red Ensign as its House Flag, and even then it was defaced with the letters 'H.B.C.'. A few firms include the modern Union Flag not in the canton of their House Flag but as part of its design. It appears, for example, at the centre of the red and white flag of Glen Line Ltd. (red funnels with a black top); the pendant bearing a white Maltese Cross represents a custom dating from the days of the clipper ships and indicated that a ship was speeding home from China with a cargo of tea; it was essential to get this home as soon as possible, because tea quickly loses its flavour in the hold of a ship. (Plate V, figures 6 and 3.)

Many of the early steamships still used sails, and as these might conceal the funnel such vessels might fly with their house flag a special pendant known as a 'steam cornet'—a term formerly signifying a tapering flag.

An historical event older than the introduction of the earliest form of the Red Ensign, the Wars of the Roses, was commemorated in two house flags. The White Rose of York was displayed on the green flag of the North Yorkshire Shipping Co. Ltd. (black funnels), the Red Rose of Lancashire upon a white circle on the blue flag (and upon the white band of the red black-topped funnels) of the Red Rose Navigation Co. Ltd. (Plate V, figures 4 and 5.) The former was a subsidiary of the Bolton Steam Shipping Co., Ltd., whose red flag bears a white diamond with the letters 'F.B.' (the initials of Sir Frederick Bolton, founder of the Company and grandfather of the present Chairman) in red. Similar diamonds now appear on their red-banded black funnel (Plate V, figure 12).

Two firms, in token of assistance rendered to the French Government, were allowed to fly the French tricolour, defaced by a British emblem on the white stripe. Ships of P. Henderson & Co. (black funnels) flew it reversed (the red in the hoist) with a small Union Flag on the white; those of the J. & P. Hutchison Line (black funnels with a white band) flew it unreversed, the white stripe marked with a red and green thistle. This permission was granted for services rendered respectively during the Crimean and Franco-Prussian Wars (Plate V, figures 7 and 8).

B.F.—4

It is natural that many House Flags should bear Scottish emblems, for the Clyde is one of the greatest shipbuilding centres, and Scots engineers have earned a world-wide fame. One historic Scottish symbol used on House Flags is the rampant lion, though without the tressure which makes it part of the royal emblem. Red on a white diamond, the Scottish lion appears on the red House Flag of the Clan Line Steamers Ltd. (black funnels with two red bands). Crowned, and holding a globe of the world between its paws, gold on a red field, it forms the Cunard House Flag (Plate V, figure 10; Plate VI, figure 1).

British Railways formerly displayed their emblem, a lion astride of a wheel, on a blue flag crossed by red and white diagonals. The House Flag of British Rail is blue and is crossed horizontally by two broad white lines, representing railway tracks, with arrow-like markings pointing in opposite directions. The same emblem appears on their black-tipped red funnels, and for use on land, upon a red flag (Plate V, figure 11).

The Cunard Steamship Company (Cunard White Star) formerly combined the flags of the Cunard and White Star Lines. Those which were originally Cunard ships (red funnels with a black top) flew the lion above the star; the former White Star ships (yellow funnels with a black top) flew a tapering burgee, red with a white star, above the lion (Plate VI, figure 1).

The Union Castle Line, also formed by the union of two shipping companies, shows this not by using two flags but by combining their emblems on one. The Castle Line used to fly the Scottish saltire, white on a blue field, but with a white diamond bearing the letter 'C' at its centre; the Union Line flew the St. Patrick's saltire, red on a white field inside a blue edging. The letter 'C' and the blue edging have vanished, and Union Castle ships (red funnels with a black top) now fly a blue flag with a red saltire inside a white saltire, and a white diamond at the centre (Plate VI, figure 2).

The General Steam Navigation Co. Ltd. (funnels black) is best known for continental and European trading. Its original aim, however, was to trade all over the world as is shown by the picture of the globe, red on a white field, on its flag and funnel.

Flag and Funnel of General Steam Navigation Co. Ltd.

Though it may not look heraldic, the flag of the Peninsular & Oriental Line (funnels black or yellow) is derived from the standards of two royal families. The Company gained the first half of its name by trading with Spain and Portugal, and during a period of war and insurrection it rendered assistance to the Queens of both countries. The P. & O. flag, of envelope design, is accordingly in four colours, blue and white from the royal arms of Portugal, red and yellow from those of Spain (Plate VI, figure 3).

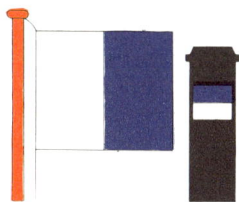

1. Cunard-Brocklebank Ltd.

2. Muscovy Company

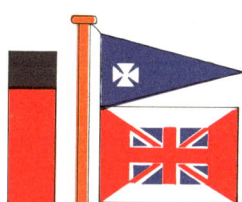

3. Glen Line Ltd.

4. North Yorkshire
   Shipping Co. Ltd.

5. Red Rose Navigation
   Co. Ltd.

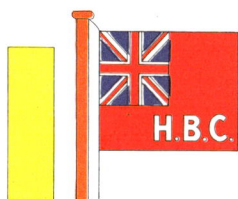

6. Hudson's Bay Co.
   (obsolete)

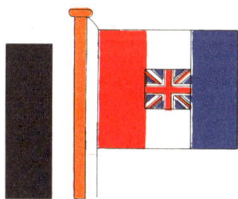

7. P. Henderson & Co.

8. J. & P. Hutchison
   Line Ltd.

9. British Petroleum
   Tanker Co. Ltd.

10. Clan Line Steamers
    Ltd.

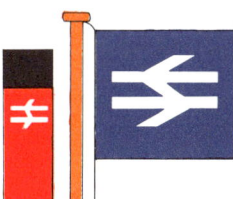

11. British Rail.

12. Bolton Steam
    Shipping Co. Ltd.

Plate V

One British line, the Shaw, Savill & Albion Co. Ltd. (buff funnels with a black top) flies what used actually to be a national flag. Its House Flag is a St. George's Cross, red on a white field, but its canton is a smaller cross, also of St. George's type, red on a blue field with a white star in each of its quarters. This resembles what was at one time the flag of New Zealand (Plate VI, figure 4).

The plain St. George's Cross, red on white, is one of the flags of the Royal Navy which merchant vessels are forbidden to use. The sailing-ship *Sir Edward Pagett*, belonging to a firm which no longer exists, Green and Wigram, hoisted this flag in 1824, but when she reached Spithead the Port-

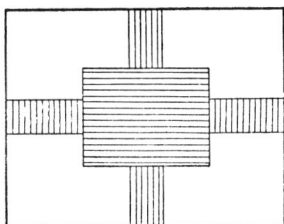

House Flag of Green and Wigram   Green's Blackwall Line

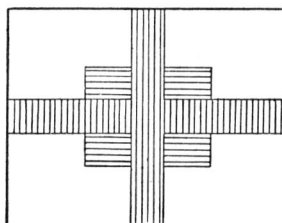

Admiral indignantly ordered it to be struck. Thereupon her captain, equally indignant, is said to have picked up a pair of sailor's breeches, cut a patch from their seat, pinned it over the centre of the flag, and re-hoisted it. Thus the firm gained its House Flag, a red cross with a blue square over its centre, on a white field. This flag is now flown by the Federal Steam Navigation Co. Ltd., who also place the same design below the black tops of their red funnels (Plate VI, figure 5). A partner of the original firm, when he formed a separate company, varied the design by placing the blue square under the red cross; this flag is no longer flown at sea, however, for Green's Blackwall Line has ceased business.

The flag of Canadian Pacific Ships displays, in green and white, symbols of stability, motion, and world-wide activity; the same device also appears on the green funnels (Plate VI, figure 6).

The white stag on a red field shown on the flag and black funnel of Stag Line, Ltd. is derived from the coat of arms of the Company's founder (Plate VI, figure 7).

The firm of Alfred Holt & Co., when they took over their first ship, found that a blue line had been painted round its hull—an old custom to mark the recent death of its owner. The spare paint was used to paint the funnel, and thus the Blue Funnel Line got its name. The firm's initials, 'A.H.', appear in black in the white diamond on its blue flag. The Blue Star Line is similarly named from the emblem, which appears both on the firm's red tapering burgee and on its red funnels below the black top with the white line at its base—a blue star in a white circle (Plate VI, figures 8 and 9).

Some House Flags symbolize the regions with which the vessels trade. For instance, the Black Swan of Western Australia is shown at the centre of a gold cross on a blue field upon the flag and the black-topped yellow funnel of the Australind Steam Shipping Co. Ltd. (Plate VI, figure 12.)

Many shipbuilding companies also have their own House Flags. Govan Shipbuilders Ltd. place their initials upon a St. Andrew's cross. The initials of Harland & Wolff appear, in yellow, on a black, yellow-bordered diamond at the centre of a flag of 'envelope' design, white and red. Vickers Ltd. display the badge from their coat-of-arms on a blue flag with a yellow border (Plate VI, figure 10). One company, Cammell Laird Shipbuilders Ltd.,

Former Flag of Cammell
Laird Shipbuilders Ltd.

formerly used heraldic punning: on a white field appeared, in red, the firm's initials and their former trade-mark—a camel. Their present flag is shown on Plate VI, figure 11.

The House Flag of the shipbuilder is flown over a merchant vessel—though not nowadays over a ship of the Royal Navy —at her launching, together with that of the shipping firm for which she is intended.

It is also flown during her speed trial, but as soon as this is satisfactorily completed it is lowered, and that of her owners is raised, to show that they have taken her over.

A red flag—or a thin sheet of metal resembling a flag—with a white spot at its centre, shows that the vessel is carrying or unloading or loading oil. The oil-tanker firms also have their own House Flags: that of the Shell Tankers Co. displays the well-known Shell emblem, in yellow, in a white circle upon a red flag; and, also in yellow, on the red funnel. That of the B.P. Tanker Co. places the letters B.P. in yellow, on a green shield, upon a white, green-bordered flag; the red funnel has a black top, below which the shield bearing these letters appears on a white square (Plate V, figure 9).

Forbidden to fly the Royal Navy's emblem, the Union Jack, at the bow, some merchant vessels fly the Pilot Jack instead. The Canadian Pacific Company uses as its Jack a small copy of its House Flag.

Following the practice of the Royal Navy, the Master of a merchant ship is often called her Captain. Some firms carry Naval practice farther by giving their senior captain the title of Commodore and allowing him to fly a Commodore's Burgee at the mainmast. This must not resemble the Broad Pendant of a Commodore, R.N.; it usually consists of the Company's House Flag with its fly cut into a swallow-tail.

Both the Royal Navy and the Merchant Navy 'dress ship' on special occasions by flying strings of flags from mast-head to deck. National flags are unsuitable for this purpose: to fly one above the other would

1. Cunard White Star Ltd.

2. Union Castle Mail Steamship Co. Ltd.

3. Peninsular & Oriental

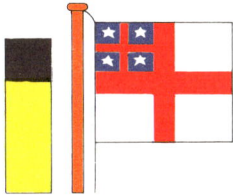

4. Shaw, Savill & Albion Co. Ltd.

5. Federal Steam Navigation Co. Ltd.

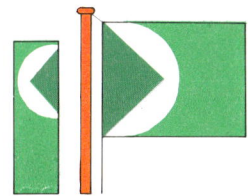

6. Canadian Pacific Ltd.

7. Stag Line Ltd.

8. Alfred Holt & Co.

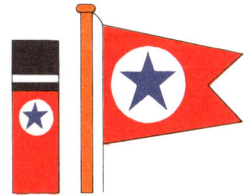

9. Blue Star Line Ltd.

10. Vickers Ltd.

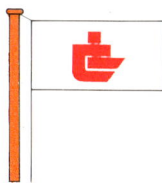

11. Cammell Laird Shipbuilders Ltd.

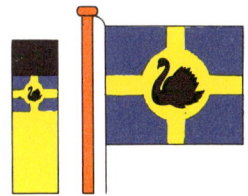

12. Australind Steam Shipping Co. Ltd.

Plate VI

insult the country whose flag was the lower. The flags commonly used in dressing ship are the International Code of Signals, arranged not to spell out messages but simply to make an attractive display; the Royal Navy places the square code flags alternately with triangular flags or pendants. This is known as 'dressing overall', but when at sea a vessel may 'dress with mast-head flags' more simply by flying national flags at her mast-heads, her ensign, and her jack.

THE DEVELOPMENT OF THE RED DUSTER

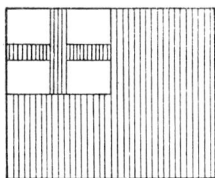

1674

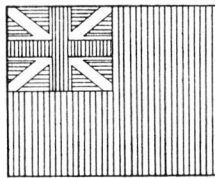

1707

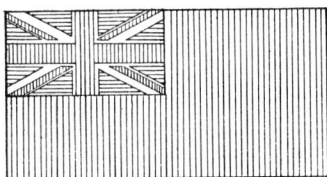

1801

The Red Ensign is one of the oldest British flags. Affectionately spoken of by seamen as the 'Red Duster', it is probably the most widely known of all the world's flags; in foreign flag-books it, and not the Union, has often appeared as the English emblem. It flies over every type of vessel, from liners and trim private yachts to fishing-boats and the humble tramp steamers which carry articles of commerce around our shores—those which John Masefield so well describes in his poem *Cargoes*:

> *Dirty British coaster with a salt-caked smoke-stack*
> *Butting through the Channel in the mad March days*
> *With a cargo of Tyne coal,*
> *Road-rails, pig-lead,*
> *Firewood, iron-ware, and cheap tin trays.*

8

OFFICIAL AND CIVIC FLAGS

> *. . . in the air*
> *A thousand streamers floated fair*
> *Various in shape, device and hue,*
> *Green, sanguine, purple, red and blue,*
> *Broad, narrow, swallow-tailed and square.*

SIR WALTER SCOTT: MARMION

BRITAIN has many flags besides the Royal Standards and the National Flags. A number of responsible officers and of organizations which serve the public have emblems with centuries of tradition behind them, emblems recognized by the College of Arms and conforming to the heraldic rules.

With few exceptions, representatives of Her Majesty the Queen are authorized to fly the national emblem, the Union Flag, with a special badge at its centre. The badge of the Governor of Northern Ireland is a shield bearing the St. George's Cross (*not* St. Patrick's) red on white; at the centre of the Cross is the Imperial Crown above a six-pointed white star on which is the 'Red Hand of Ulster', famous in Irish legend (Plate III, figure 3).

The Governors General of the different Dominions no longer fly, as formerly, the Union Flag with the Dominion badge. Their flag is now dark blue and bears the Royal Crest, a lion surmounting a crown and the Dominion's name.

Flag of the Governor General of Canada

Officers of the Diplomatic Service, who represent Britain in the more important foreign countries, fly the Union Flag with the Royal Arms at its centre in a white circle surrounded by a garland. Consular Officers—Britain's representatives in the smaller countries—also fly the Union Flag when ashore, charged with a Tudor Crown on a white circle (no garland); when they are afloat their flag is the Blue Ensign with the Royal Arms in its fly.

The Queen's representatives in Britain, the Lords Lieutenants of the Counties, fly the Union Flag with a badge showing a gold sword placed horizontally, pointing away from the hoist, below a crown. The Queen's

Harbour Masters fly the Union Flag surrounded by a white border, and with a crown and the letters 'Q.H.M.' on a white circle.

Government buildings fly the Union Flag, undefaced by any badge, on

OFFICIAL BADGES

Queen's Harbour Master

Diplomatic Officer

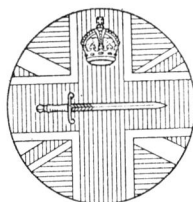

Lord Lieutenant of County

Consular Officer
Afloat

Consular Officer
on Shore

such official occasions as the Queen's Birthday. Ships employed by Government departments hoist either a square Blue Ensign flown as a Jack, or a Blue Ensign of the usual type defaced in its fly by a special badge. Most of these official badges symbolize the work of the department they represent.

Formed in 1964, the Ministry of Defence has at present no flag; over its Headquarters fly the flags of the three Services whose work it co-ordinates: the White Ensign, the Union Flag, and the R.A.F. Ensign. The car-flag of the Chief of Defence Staff combines the colours and emblems of the Services: it is a horizontal tricolour of dark blue for the Royal Navy; red for the Army; and light blue for the Royal Air Force; at its centre a composite badge unites the anchor and cable and the crossed swords with the R.A.F. Eagle.

Royal Fleet Auxiliary Vessels, though employed by the Admiralty, do

Chief of Defence Staff

not fly the Admiralty Flag, the emblem which shows that the Queen is aboard; their badge is also an anchor, but it appears in the fly of the Blue Ensign. A crown above a fish surrounded by a yellow ring is the badge of the Ministry of Agriculture, Fisheries and Food. A crown above an upright anchor between the letters 'S.F.' surrounded by a wreath of thistles is that of the Department of Agriculture and Fisheries for Scotland. The flag of the Forestry Commission bears

Forestry Commission

brown stripes on a green field, the colour of the soil and the trees; below the Royal Crown appear the words 'Forestry Commission'.

Vessels employed in the North Sea Fisheries fly a pendant, quartered blue and yellow. A white pendant edged with red and bearing a crown above a portcullis and chains is the flag of the Customs Commissioners. A blue flag containing a white and red oblong is flown by Examination Vessels. There is also a special Royal Mail Pendant.

Of the badges in the fly of the Blue Ensign, the simplest was that of H.M. Customs, a Tudor Crown. This has now been changed to the traditional emblem of the Customs, a gold portcullis, chains, and crown. The most picturesque is that of the Department of Trade and Industry: a

Post Office

sailing-ship at sea. The most spectacular is that of the Post Office (which is, of course, no longer a Government department): a white figure of Father Time with his scythe, but with a flash of lightning shattering his hour-glass. The most symbolic was that of the Ministry of Transport, whose flag replaced the Red Ensign on the troopships, emigrant ships and official launches for which the Ministry was responsible: it was a Blue Ensign, defaced by a badge consisting of an anchor and wheel surmounted by a crown.

During the Middle Ages the Cinque Ports, situated on the coast of Kent

Customs Commissioners

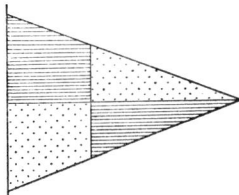

North Sea Fisheries

Royal Mail

Ministry of Agriculture, Fisheries and Food

Department of Trade and Industry

Department of Agriculture and Fisheries for Scotland

Customs

Ministry of Transport

Royal Fleet Auxiliary Badge

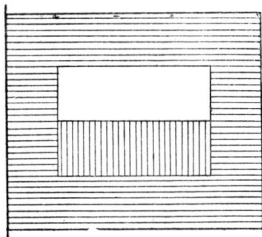

Examination Vessels

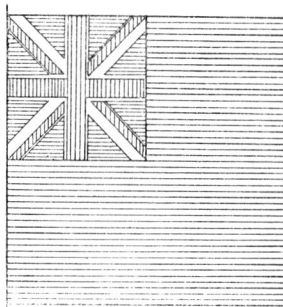

Public Offices Jack

and Sussex, had the duty of providing ships for national defence. In return the kings of England granted them special privileges, including the right to include in their flag one of the most curious emblems known to heraldry.

The Cinque Ports flag is quartered, with its second and third quarters divided vertically into halves. In the first quarter are three pictures of Dover Castle, one large and two small; in the fourth is a still larger picture of the Castle; all are red and yellow on a blue field. In the left half of the second quarter is a yellow square containing an anchor below a peer's coronet; in that of the third quarter is a sailing-ship, red on yellow. In the right half of each of these quarters, arranged one above the other, are the heads and forequarters of three lions united to the halves of three ships. For this strange emblem the heralds have an equally strange term: the lions and ships are *dimidiated* (Plate VII, figure 1).

Founded by Henry VIII to promote commerce and navigation, Trinity House appoints and licenses pilots for Britain's coast and supervises the lighthouses, lightships, and buoys of England and Wales. Its Jack is the St. George's Cross, red on white; in each of the four quarters is the picture of a sailing-ship of ancient design at sea (Plate VII, figure 2). This emblem of the Cross and four ships also appears in the fly of the Trinity House Red Ensign and in the Trinity House Red Burgee. The special flag flown by the Master of Trinity House, who is often a member of the Royal Family, contains the same fourfold emblem twice; not only does it constitute the flag, it is also repeated at the centre on a shield surmounted by the head and forequarters of a rampant lion.

Many counties, cities, and towns have their civic flags, based on their coats of arms. The City of London, as the capital of England, naturally uses the traditional English emblem, the St. George's Cross, in its arms and flag. The emblem, red on a white field, in the canton represents not, as is sometimes said, the dagger which slew Wat Tyler—the arms are too ancient for that—but the sword which beheaded St. Paul. This refers to a tradition that St. Paul actually visited London and preached on the top of Ludgate Hill, where the great Cathedral now stands (Plate VII, figure 3).

A number of public bodies which are associated with or have their headquarters in London also base their flags on the St. George's Cross. The flag of the London County Council, modern though it was, was designed by the heralds: the Cross displayed a leopard, similar to that on the Royal Coat of Arms; it was surmounted by a crown of *mural* type, the heraldic sign for a city, and was placed above six blue and white *wavy bars*, the heraldic symbol for water. The whole device signified that London is the royal capital of England and stands on a river (Plate VII, figure 4).

The L.C.C. was merged in 1965 into the Greater London Council, whose emblem does *not* include the St. George's Cross; instead, it displays above the wavy bars a Saxon crown, gold on a red field, to symbolize the ancient Saxon associations of London.

1. Cinque Ports

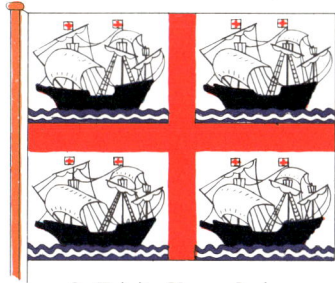

2. Trinity House Jack

3. City of London

4. London County Council

5. Port of London Authority

6. Thames Conservators

7. British Broadcasting Corporation

8. Royal National Lifeboat Institution

Plate VII

The Port of London Authority, which controls the mighty traffic of the great London docks, possesses several flags. Vessels on which the Chairman of the Authority embarks fly its House Flag, the design of which is the

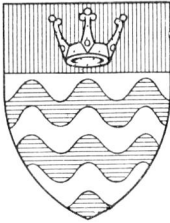

Greater London
Council Badge

Port of London
Authority Badge

St. George's Cross with the P.L.A. Arms at its centre: the head and shoulders of a man (St. Paul) carrying a sword and a scroll emerging from the top of a building which represents the Tower of London (Plate VII, figure 5). The Blue Ensign flown by P.L.A. vessels on service in the docks or on the Thames is defaced in its fly by a gold sea-lion grasping a trident.

The Thames Conservancy, which is responsible for the condition and traffic of the River Thames above Teddington, flies on its launches a flag bearing its Arms at the centre of the St. George's Cross. These consist of two shields, one bearing the Arms of the City of London and the other those of Trinity House; an anchor and a sceptre are behind them, and a crown above (Plate VII, figure 6). Thames Conservancy Officers, when on patrol or regulating traffic at such events as regattas, fly a simpler flag bearing the words 'THAMES CONSERVANCY' one above the other on a red field. When the Conservators are on board, however, the flag displaying the arms is flown at the stern while at the bows is a pendant bearing the letters 'T.C.'.

The University of London flies a flag bearing its arms: at the centre of the St. George's Cross is a heraldic rose, surrounded by rays below an Imperial Crown. Above the Cross, an open book with gold clasps is represented on a blue field.

In its work of organizing the insurance of shipping, Lloyd's has its own chain of signal stations; it is distinct from Lloyd's Register of Shipping which classifies merchant ships as seaworthy—'A1 at Lloyd's' is the finest description a vessel can have. So important a service does it perform that it was once allowed to use the White Ensign, defaced with its arms. This practice ceased at the beginning of this

Flag of London University

century, however, and its signal stations now fly the Blue Ensign with the Lloyd's badge in the fly, a shield bearing the Arms of London City, above an anchor, gold on a blue field.

Some of the Lloyd's Agents fly this flag, though without authority, above their office buildings; it is not flown at sea because Lloyd's own no vessels. When the Agents go out to board ships which need assistance, and when members of Lloyd's sail their own private yachts, they fly Lloyd's Burgee for Boats. This is a white pendant bearing a St. George's Cross, whose arms run inside a blue cross with broader arms; it has the Lloyd's badge in the canton.

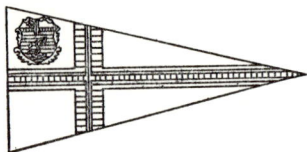

Lloyd's Burgee for Boats

The flag of the Royal National Lifeboat Institution bears a similar device, a red St. George's Cross edged with blue on a white field. In each of its quarters appear the letters 'R.N.L.I.' and at its centre is a crown above an anchor. It is flown on lifeboats and lifeboat-houses, and also on the Institution's London office and its depot at Boreham Wood (Plate VII, figure 8). The lifeboats may also fly a Red Ensign with a similar device in the fly.

Churches, as well as secular buildings, are entitled to fly flags. Westminster Abbey is, indeed, entitled to fly several, not only the Royal Standard when the Queen is in or near the Abbey, but the St. George's Cross on St. George's Day, a flag bearing St. Peter's emblem, the Crossed Keys, on Church festivals, and its own flag, a design including *martlets*—heraldic birds resembling swifts. (See Appendix 3.)

A warrant issued by the Earl Marshal at the request of the Archbishop of Canterbury declares the flag proper to be flown by any church within

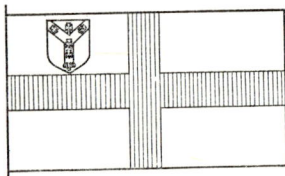

Church Flag

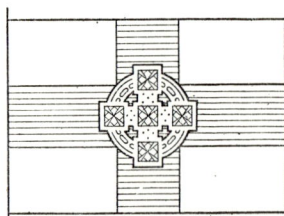

Flag of the Welsh Churches

the provinces of Canterbury and York to be the Cross of St. George, and in the first quarter an escutcheon of the Arms of the See in which the church is ecclesiastically situated. A few churches, however, prefer simply to fly the St. George's Cross. St. Martin-in-the-Fields, Trafalgar Square, flies the White Ensign on appropriate occasions.

Churches in the province of Wales are now authorized to fly a white flag charged with a royal blue cross of St. George type and displaying at its centre a Celtic Cross in gold.

The flag of the British Broadcasting Corporation contains the same design as appears on the shield in the B.B.C.'s coat of arms. On a blue field representing the ether, the Earth is shown floating among the seven planets: a golden ring encircling the globe symbolizes broadcasting (Plate VII, figure 7).

The Second World War produced two new ensigns. That of the Civil Defence Service has the Union Flag in the canton: its second and third quarters are yellow and its fourth quarter is blue. Its fourth quarter may bear the Crown and the letters 'C.D.' in gold. The National Fire Service also had its ensign, with the Union Flag in the canton; its second and third quarters were blue and its fourth quarter red (Plate IV, figures 7 and 8). These, however, were land flags; boats belonging to the Fire Service wore the Blue Ensign which showed they were Government vessels, with the N.F.S. badge in the fly.

Similarly, the taking over of the coal fields by the National Coal Board produced a new flag, which was hoisted above the pit-heads. It bore the initials of the Board on a blue field.

The Royal Geographical Society has supported many expeditions to various parts of the world. Its House Flag has a St. George's Cross in the hoist. The fly consists of two horizontal stripes, white above blue, and in the centre is the Society's badge, a globe of the earth, around which runs the Society's name. Above this is a crown.

Royal Geographical Society

The flag was carried on Captain Scott's ship the *Discovery* to the Antarctic ice and is now preserved in the Society's House.

The National Maritime Museum and the Old Royal Observatory fly the former Navy Board flag: three anchors, in gold, on a red field.

The launches with which the Thames Division of the Metropolitan Police patrols the river use the Blue Ensign. In its fly a star bearing the words 'Metropolitan Police' and the Royal initials 'E. R. II' is surmounted by the Royal Crown.

In 1967 the Metropolitan Police

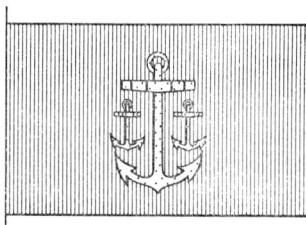

National Maritime Museum

were granted their standard and flag; in the canton is displayed the emblem of the City of Westminster, where the Force was first established

in 1829, the portcullis and chains; in the fly the Force's star appears, in white on blue, surmounted by the Royal Crown.

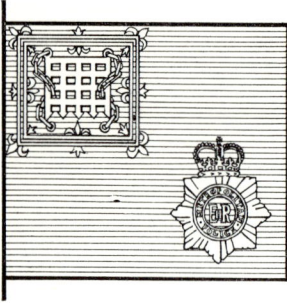

Metropolitan Police

The Union Flag which flies over the Victoria Tower of the Houses of Parliament may indicate, as when flown over other Government buildings, a day of national rejoicing. On other occasions, however, it is the sign, by day, that Parliament is sitting (at night this is indicated by a light over Big Ben). When the Sovereign makes a state visit to Parliament it is replaced by the Royal Standard.

9

FLAGS OF THE UNITED STATES

'Tis the star-spangled banner; oh, long may it wave
O'er the land of the free and the home of the brave.

THE AMERICAN NATIONAL ANTHEM

JUST as several foreign emblems have appeared on the British Royal Standard, so a number of European flags have flown over North America. The earliest of these may have been the Viking Raven Flag, taken across the Atlantic by Leif Ericsson nearly a thousand years ago. The flag unfurled by Columbus over the West Indies was the Royal Standard of Spain: it quartered the arms of Castile, a gold castle on a red field, with those of Leon, a red lion rampant on a white field.

The Dutch, who established a colony in America, the New Netherlands (its capital, New Amsterdam, is now called New York), flew first their older flag, of orange, white, and blue, and later their modern red, white, and blue; each bore on the white strip the initials of a trading company. The Swedes, who founded a colony on the Delaware River, flew their gold cross on a blue field.

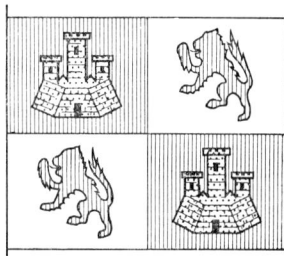

Flag unfurled by Columbus

The French hoisted several flags over their American colonies: one was the Royal Banner, the heraldic Lilies. The French Republican Flag, the blue, white, and red Tricolour, later flew over Louisiana. California and Texas, when they belonged to Mexico, flew that country's flag.

Tree of Liberty

To establish an English claim on the New World, Sir Walter Raleigh hoisted the St. George's Cross over the land he hoped to colonize in Virginia, but it did not fly there long. It was the colonial enterprise of the East India Company and the Virginia Company in the early seventeenth century which led

Rattlesnake Flag

to the planting of the earlier Union Flag, combining the crosses of St. George and of St. Andrew, west of the Atlantic.

These crosses offended some rigid Puritans, who preferred a flag on which was represented a pine tree; this was not merely a local emblem but a symbol of democracy, for under such trees village councils debated their affairs. Some of the thirteen North American States, then under British rule, had their own flags: the strangest was that of South Carolina, a rattlesnake on a yellow field, with the motto, 'Don't Tread on Me'.

A flag, displaying a silver arm issuing from a cloud and brandishing a sword, with a Latin motto meaning, 'Conquer or Die', is believed to have

'Conquer or Die'

been carried into action by the American Militia at the Battle of Concord, which began the War of Independence. This emblem is based on that of the Cavalry Standard of the Parliamentary Forces during the English Civil War.

The ensign of the East India Company, the most famous of British trading companies, bore in its fly thirteen red and white horizontal stripes; in the canton was first the St. George's Cross, later replaced by the first Union Flag. This ensign, flown by ships which carried on a thriving trade with America, was well known; after it had been carried away in triumph from the 'Boston Tea Party' of 1773, some say, it became the American National Flag.

The Union in its canton showed that, though they had taken up arms in defence of their rights, the colonists still regarded themselves as loyal subjects of the British King, while its thirteen stripes well symbolized the unity of their thirteen States. The colonists called it the Union Flag, the Grand Union Flag, the Great Union Flag—and also the Cambridge Flag, after the town in Massachusetts near which George Washington ceremonially unfurled it. It is, however, uncertain whether this flag was actually copied from that of the East India Company, or whether it was devised independently by placing six horizontal white stripes upon the fly of the British Red Ensign (Plate VIII, figure 2).

When, however, the Americans decided to break away from the Mother Country, they objected to the British Union in the canton and decided to replace it by their own emblem. To use a State flag might arouse jealousy; and the old 'Liberty Tree', being green, would not harmonize with the red stripes. The American Congress at last adopted a flag retaining the thirteen stripes, but placed thirteen stars, white on a blue field, in the canton, to represent the thirteen seceding States (Plate VIII, figure 3).

A new country having been formed on earth, it seemed appropriate to use as its symbol a new constellation in the sky. The new design had the further advantage that it complimented the leader whom America still delights to honour: three red stars at the top of a white shield, with two red bars below, appeared on the arms of George Washington. Heraldic stars have six points, and the 'stars' on his shield and on the American flag, having only five points, are really *mullets*, the rowels of spurs. None the less, the flag of the U.S.A. has always been called the Stars and Stripes.

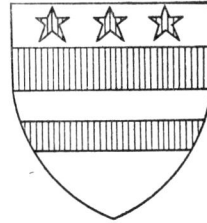

George Washington's
Coat of Arms

At first a new star was added to the canton, and a new stripe to the fly, to symbolize the admission of a new State to the Union. The actual Star-Spangled Banner which, as it flew over Fort McHenry during the Second Anglo-American War of 1812–14, inspired Francis Scott Key to write the American National Anthem, bore fifteen stars, arranged in five rows of three, and fifteen red and white stripes.

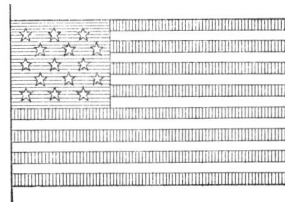

As the nation grew, however, it was clear that the stripes would become too numerous, and the arrangement of the stars too elaborate, for the flag to be effective. Congress therefore decided that one star should be added for every new State, but that the number of stripes should revert to thirteen, one for each of the thirteen original States. The stars were arranged in horizontal rows.

The Star-Spangled Banner

In 1861 the American Civil War threatened to remove some of these emblems from the flag. A growing dispute about Negro slavery induced some of the Southern States to secede from the Union; President Abraham Lincoln opened war on them in order to keep his country united. His forces, the Northerners, retained the Stars and Stripes: it symbolized their aim to keep both the flag and the Union it represented intact.

The Confederate (Southern) forces needed a new flag. Though they wished to break with the Union, they were still Americans, proud of the tradition of freedom for which their ancestors had fought under George Washington. Just as their ancestors had at first flown the Cambridge Flag in token of their loyalty to Britain, so the Southerners showed their faith in the American ideal by adopting a flag using the American emblem in a different form.

The earliest flag of the Southern States, the Stars and Bars, was also an ensign with a blue-and-white canton and a red-and-white field. Instead

B.F.—5

of thirteen narrow stripes, however, its fly was divided horizontally into three broad bars, red above and below and white between. The stars in the canton were generally arranged not in horizontal rows but, like those on one of the original Stars and Stripes, in a circle; they successively numbered from seven to thirteen, to represent the seceding States (Plate VIII, figure 4).

The new flag, indeed, so much resembled the Stars and Stripes as to risk confusion in battle. The Southern States therefore chose another flag: this, though not an ensign, still kept the old colours and the old emblem of white stars on a blue field but arranged them differently. This second flag, the Southern Cross, had nothing to do with the star-group of that name; it was so called because it was the cross of the Southern States. It generally consisted of a blue saltire with a white fimbriation on a red field, the saltire bearing thirteen white stars (Plate VIII, figure 5). The whole flag was bordered in white.

For use at sea, the Southern Cross was later converted into an ensign by being placed in the canton of a larger flag with a plain white field. Finally, for greater distinctness, a broad red stripe was run vertically down the fly. Then the victory of the Northern States made the Southern Cross go out of official use and converted it into the emblem of a lost cause.

This maintained the Stars and Stripes as the National Flag—it is also the Merchant Flag and the Ensign—of the United States. Additional stars continued to be added to the canton to symbolize the admission of new states to the Union, and the flag came into its present form in 1960, after Alaska and Hawaii had become States. Its field still consists of thirteen horizontal stripes, seven red and six white; in its canton are fifty stars, white on a blue field (Plate VIII, figure 1). Fringed in gold and having cords and tassels, it is used by military units as the National Colour, together with their own Regimental or Organizational Colours.

Ships of the U.S. Navy wear a Jack at the bow consisting of a blue flag bearing fifty stars similar to the canton of the Stars and Stripes; this is also called the Union Jack of the United States. The Pendant now has seven stars, arranged horizontally, white on blue, in the hoist; the fly is divided horizontally, red above white.

President's Standard

Like our own Queen, the U.S. President, as the head of a Sovereign State, is entitled to fly his own personal Standard. Its design—which remains almost unchanged as President follows President—resembles that on the U.S. Seal: an eagle grasping the symbols of war and peace, thirteen arrows and an olive-branch; thirteen white and red stripes run vertically down a blue-topped shield; above and by the eagle's head are thirteen white stars; fifty

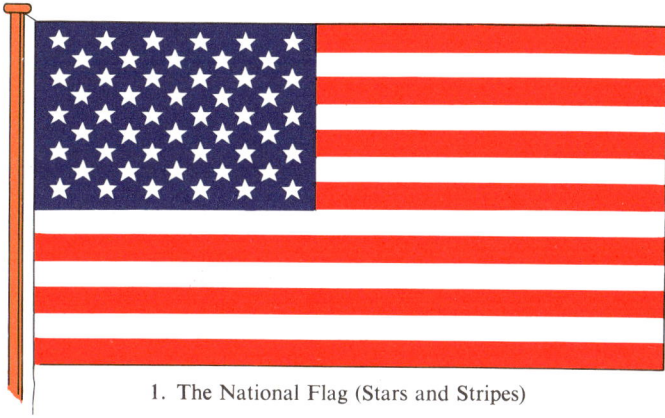

1. The National Flag (Stars and Stripes)

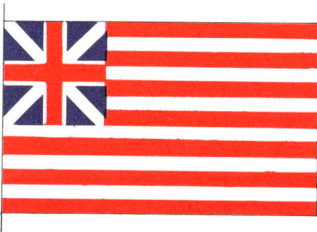

2. The Cambridge Flag

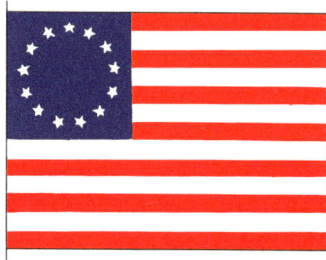

3. Original Stars and Stripes
(variant)

4. The Confederate Stars and Bars
(variant)

5. The Confederate Southern Cross
(variant)

Plate VIII

stars surround it; the field is blue; the Latin motto means 'One out of Many'.

The Secretary of the U.S. Navy flies a flag showing a foul anchor, between four stars, white on a blue field; the flag of the Assistant Secretary bears a similar design, blue on white. The Admirals' flags are blue, with the rank indicated by white stars; unlike those of the Royal Navy, but like those of most other countries, these flags indicate a higher rank by increasing the number of stars. A Fleet Admiral's flag bears five stars arranged in the form of a pentagon; an Admiral's, four in diamond shape; a Vice-Admiral's three; a Rear Admiral's two; a Commodore's one, on a tapering burgee. A similar practice is followed in the Army, where the rank of General Officers is indicated by red flags bearing white stars. That of a General of the Army bears five stars; a General's four; a Lieutenant-General's three; a Major-General's two; and a Brigadier's one. A General of the U.S. Air Force flies a blue flag on which are four white stars arranged in a straight line.

The U.S. Navy has its own Naval Ceremonial Flag and the U.S. Army

Army Ceremonial Flag

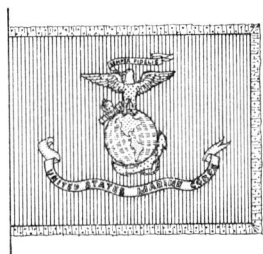

Marine Corps
Ceremonial Flag

Naval Ceremonial Flag

and Marines also have their own flags; the latter displays a globe of the western hemisphere.

The flag of the U.S. Naval Reserve is a tapering burgee; its blue field bears the eagle above two crossed anchors in white, with a white shield decorated with blue stars and red vertical stripes. The Coastguard Flag is an ensign, with a blue eagle, a red and white shield, and thirteen blue stars in the canton and sixteen vertical stripes in the fly. The Consular Flag bears the letter 'C' within a circle of thirteen stars, white on a blue field. The flags of the U.S. Naval Militia were blue and yellow. The Naval Church Pendant, a blue Latin Cross placed horizontally on a white field, is flown

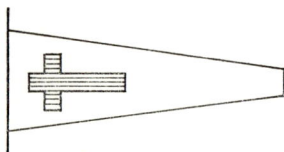

U.S. Church Pendant

above the Stars and Stripes during Divine Service and is the only flag allowed to occupy such a position.

The flag of the Secretary of Defence bears the U.S. National Emblem, the eagle, in its centre; in each corner is a star and the field is blue.

The fifty States in the Union have their own flags, the designs of which are as varied as the colonial badges on the British ensigns. One has different designs on the two sides. Many of them are based on the emblems of their official seals; some, however, deserve special mention. All these flags are rectangular, with one exception: the flag of Ohio is a tapering

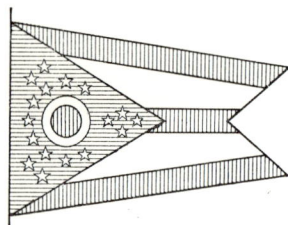

Ohio

burgee striped red and white; a blue triangle in the hoist displays seventeen stars—this was the seventeenth State to join the Union—around a red letter 'O' fimbriated with white.

Other States put stars on their flags to indicate the order in which they were admitted to the Union. Thus Arkansas flies a flag bearing twenty-five stars to show that it was the twenty-fifth State to be admitted; Tennessee, the sixteenth State, places on its flag three stars only—it was the third after the original Thirteen.

The flags of several States are as heraldic as those of Europe. That of Maryland is based on the arms of an ancient family. That of Rhode Island bears an anchor surrounded by stars, that of Louisiana a pelican feeding its young, that of Indiana a golden torch. Two flags, those of

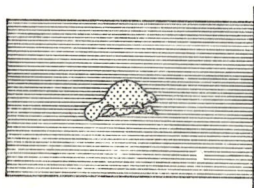

Oregon (reverse)

North Dakota and Illinois, bear eagles resembling that on the United States seal. The square flag of Alabama bears what is called a 'crimson St. Andrew's Cross'—it is really the saltire of St. Patrick!

Like some of the Commonwealth countries, a few of the American States have flags representing the characteristic animal or plant of the region. On the flag

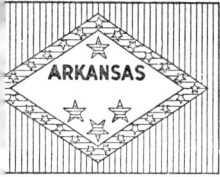

Arkansas

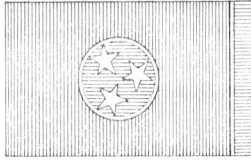

Tennessee

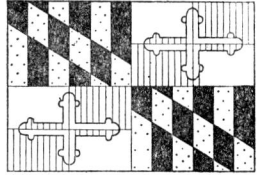

Maryland

Rhode Island

Louisiana

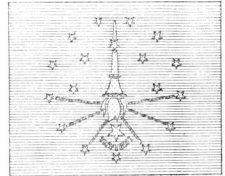

Indiana

California

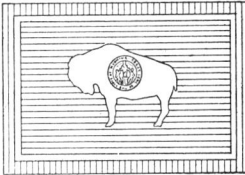

Wyoming

Oregon

Kansas

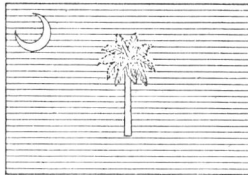

South Carolina

Kentucky

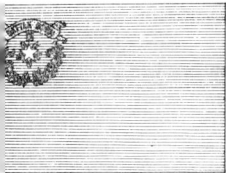

Nevada

Oklahoma

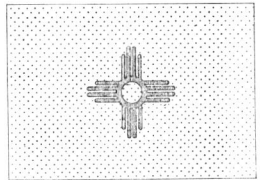

New Mexico

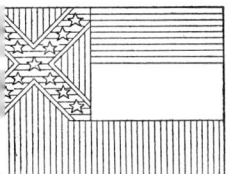

Mississippi

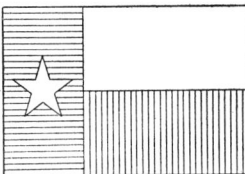

Texas

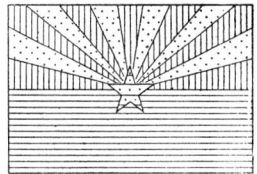

Arizona

of California it is a grizzly bear, on that of Wyoming a buffalo; on the reverse of that of Oregon is a golden beaver (the fur trade was important in the State's early development); and on the obverse the State Seal. A sunflower appears on the flag of Kansas, and a palm tree on that of South Carolina; wreaths of golden-rod and of sage-brush appear respectively on those of Kentucky and Nevada; the words 'Battle Born' on the badge of the flag of Nevada show that this region became a State during the Civil War.

The early inhabitants of America are not forgotten. Oklahoma displays on its flag an Indian warrior's shield bearing seven eagle feathers; across this is a saltire formed by the Indian and the classical emblems of peace— the peace-pipe crossed by the olive-branch. The circle at the centre of a cross on the flag of New Mexico is an ancient Zuñi emblem of the sun and its rays, though the colours, red and gold, come from the arms of Spain.

The flag of Massachusetts bears the State Arms, a shield depicting an Indian. Its reverse formerly displayed the traditional Liberty Tree, which now appears on the State's Maritime Flag.

Two States show on their flags their loyalty to the Southern cause in the Civil War. The ensign of Mississippi has three bars in its fly, blue, white, and red; in the canton is the old Southern Cross. The flag of Texas has two bars, white above red, in its fly; in the hoist is one white star on a blue field, a fitting emblem of the 'Lone Star State'. The flag of Arizona, identical with that formerly flown by the battleship of the same name, displays the State's emblem, the copper-coloured Star of Arizona; the field shows sunset rays of red and gold— the colours of Imperial Spain—over a blue sea. Alaska has a unique flag: gold on a dark-blue field appears the best known of all star-groups, the Great Bear.

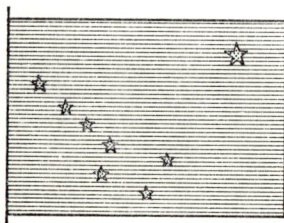

Alaska

The capital of the United States is not a State but the District of Columbia. The flag of the District is based, very appropriately, on George Washington's coat of arms: on a white field appear three red stars above two horizontal red stripes.

The State of Washington flies a green flag showing the emblem on the State Seal, which displays a portrait of George Washington.

The Yacht Flag bears the thirteen stripes. In the canton thirteen stars encircle a white foul anchor.

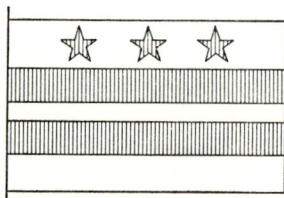

District of Columbia

Whereas our loyalty is centred upon the Throne, that of the citizens of the United States is centred upon their National Flag. Their government has issued detailed rules for its public display, and (in theory) forbids its use in any form of advertisement. The Pledge to the Flag, which is repeated on suitable occasions, declares:

'I pledge allegiance to the Flag of the United States of America, and to the Republic for which it stands, one Nation, under God, indivisible, with liberty and justice for all.'

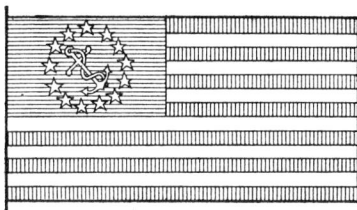

Yacht Flag

Though so different from the Union Flag of Britain, the Stars and Stripes of the U.S.A. came from one of the oldest of British ensigns. It is thus a fitting symbol for the country over which it flies, a country which was once associated with Britain, which uses a variant of our language, and which shares so many of our traditions and ideals.

In June 1966, the Stars and Stripes was carried to the moon, sealed into the tubing of the three legs of the American space craft *Surveyor* 1, and in November of that year this flag was launched into space. Badges representing the Stars and Stripes are displayed on the sleeves of the space suits worn by the American astronauts. The Stars and Stripes itself was unfurled on the moon when the crew of *Apollo XI* landed on July 20th, 1969 and later, when five other crews also landed. This did not signify, however, that the United States made any claim to territorial possession of the moon, and the crew of *Apollo XI* also left a plaque proclaiming that 'We came in peace for all mankind'.

10

FLAGS OF THE OTHER COUNTRIES OF AMERICA

They set up their ensigns for signs

THE BIBLE

THE Dominion of Canada was the first region in what was then the British Empire to attain self-government and the first to hoist its own flag—its Arms placed on the Red Ensign. This was the National Flag of Canada until 1965. When the other Commonwealth Countries first hoisted flags of their own, they too used one of the British Ensigns, usually the Blue Ensign, with a badge in the fly; and some of them still retain this type of National Flag though others, like Canada, now have flags of an individual design.

The Arms used on the first Canadian flag were granted in 1868 and combined the Arms of the four oldest Canadian provinces (Quebec, Ontario, Nova Scotia, and New Brunswick). This looked overcrowded, however, and left no space for the later provinces included in the Dominion. In 1921, therefore, a new coat of arms was designed, symbolizing not the separate provinces but Canada itself. These arms are also adapted to form the rectangular field of the Personal Flag of Queen Elizabeth II for Canada.

Canada
Personal Flag of Queen Elizabeth II

The upper part of its shield is quartered: the first three quarters are those of the Royal Standard: the three Lions of England (and Wales); the Rampant Lion and Tressure of Scotland; the Irish Harp. In the fourth quarter is the emblem removed from the Standard over a century ago, the Lilies of France; this symbolizes the French origin of many Canadians. The shield's lower part contains the Canadian emblem of three Maple Leaves, red on a white field.

In 1913, Canadian men-of-war were given permission to fly the White Ensign at the stern; they also flew the Blue Ensign, defaced with the Canadian shield, on the jackstaff. The Red Ensign similarly defaced was flown by merchantmen, as well as being the National Flag of Canada.

These arms combined a symbol of the Mother Country with the local emblem. Canada was colonized not only from Britain but from France too; for this reason the Canadian shield contains the French emblem, and the Canadian Anthem includes the words:

The lily, thistle, shamrock, rose entwine
The Maple Leaf for ever.

On February 15th, 1965, Canada hoisted its present National Flag, the red Maple Leaf on white, flanked by red stripes down the hoist and fly (Plate IX, figure 1). This flag is also the emblem of the Canadian Merchant Fleet. That of the Canadian Armed Forces is white, with the National Flag in the canton; the fly bears the emblem of the Forces, which includes crossed swords, an anchor and a flying eagle. The badge in the fly of the Canadian Naval Jack omits the crossed swords.

The flag for Anglican churches in Canada is the St. George's Cross, red on white, with a green maple leaf in each quarter.

Formerly each of the Provinces of Canada had its own version of the Red and Blue Ensigns, on which the badge of the Dominion was replaced by their respective emblems; now, however, most of the Provinces have their own provincial flags.

Quebec was originally colonized from France and was ruled by the French until it was conquered by General Wolfe; later it was also colonized from Britain. It now uses its traditional *fleurdelisé* flag: on a blue field a white cross of St. George type quarters four white fleurs-de-lis.

The former badge of Quebec was a shield displaying three fleurs-de-lis, gold on a blue field; the Lion of England, gold on red; and three Maple Leaves, green on gold.

Nova Scotia also has its own flag, on which the Royal Arms of Scotland, the Rampant Lion and Tressure, appear, red on a gold field, on a shield at the centre of a blue saltire on a white field, the St. Andrew's Cross with its colours reversed. This flag is based on the coat of arms granted by Charles I in 1626, and refers to the name of the province, which means 'New Scotland'.

The same device appeared on the former badge of Nova Scotia, except when superseded by a shield displaying a salmon (to symbolize the fishing industry) between three thistles, from 1868 to 1929.

The upper half of the flag of British Columbia displays the British Union Flag, symbolic of the province's origin as a British Colony and of its continued links with the United Kingdom; the crown at its centre represents the sovereign power which links, in free association, the British Commonwealth of Nations. Below, the sun is depicted setting over the Pacific Ocean; this symbolizes British Columbia's position as the most westerly province of Canada.

Three provinces place the Lion at the top of their emblems, New Brunswick and Prince Edward Island gold on red, Saskatchewan red on gold. On the lower part of its flag, New Brunswick symbolizes its coastal trade by a *lymphad*, an heraldic ship, black with red pendant and flags, placed above three blue and white wavy bars on a gold field. The flag of Prince

Nova Scotia

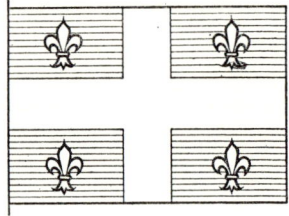

Quebec

Manitoba

Prince Edward Island

Badge of
Saskatchewan

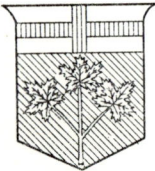

Ontario

New Brunswick

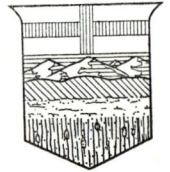

Alberta

Yukon

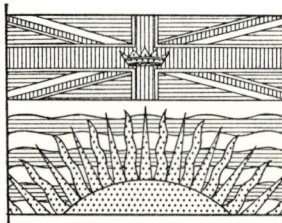

British Columbia

North-West
Territories

Edward Island shows an oak tree and three saplings, all proper on a white field; this device, like the motto on the former badge (meaning 'Small beside great'), refers to the Island itself, smallest of the Canadian provinces, in comparison with mighty Canada. Saskatchewan flies a flag divided horizontally, green above gold; in the upper hoist a shield displays a red lion on gold above three wheat sheafs, gold upon green, and in the fly appears 'the Prairie Lily' in natural colours.

Three provinces use the national emblem of England, the St. George's Cross, red on white; two display it in the fly of the Red Ensign. Below the Cross Ontario places the Canadian symbol, three Maple Leaves, gold with red veins on a green field. Manitoba shows its characteristic animal, the bison, in brown, standing on a mountain-top, on a green field. Alberta uses a landscape: a field of golden wheat, in front of a strip of green meadowland at the foot of a range of snow-covered mountains against a blue sky; this, however, appears on a flag of royal blue. The Yukon places a circle of *vair*, the heraldic symbol for fur, at the centre of a St. George's Cross at the top of its shield; below appear two red triangles, each bearing two gold circles, to represent the minerals in the mountains; separating these are narrow wavy vertical stripes, blue between

'Prairie Lily'

white, denoting the Yukon River. The crest is a malemute dog and the badge is now displayed at the centre of a vertical tricolour, forest-green, white, and lake-blue; below the shield appears a wreath of fireweed.

The North-West Territories' shield displays a horizontal wavy line, blue on white, symbolizing the famous North-West Passage through the icefields; below, gold lozenges on green represent the region's minerals, and a white fox's face represents its fur-trapping; a wavy line between indicates the 'timber line' between forest and tundra. This badge appears at the centre of a white flag with broad blue stripes in the hoist and fly; these colours represent the northern snows and the blue skies and water of the territory.

Newfoundland, which includes Labrador, has now become a Canadian province; as Britain's oldest colony, it was formerly a separate part of the Commonwealth. Its badge, which appears not on a shield but in a white circle, shows Mercury, the ancient god of travel, bringing a sailor, newly landed from a boat, to Britannia. The name above means 'New Land', and the motto means 'I bring you these gifts'. This badge, however, appears only at the centre of the Union Flag to form the distinguishing flag of the Lieutenant Governor; it no longer appears in the fly of the Blue and Red Ensigns. The official provincial flag is the Union Flag.

Though North America was colonized from the north-western countries of Europe, the place where Columbus actually landed was in Central America, and that region and South America were colonized almost entirely from Spain and Portugal. The Pope, indeed, divided the newly discovered lands between the two countries, allocating all east of a certain longitude to Portugal, all west of it to Spain. Most of the islands in the Caribbean Sea and the West Indies were, however, colonized independently by the other European countries.

The Pan-American Union, formed in 1890, includes the United States, Mexico, and much of Central and South America. It has no flag, but another emblem, the Flag of the (Latin) Races, is widely known in the New World. Its white field bears three reddish-purple crosses, said to represent the three ships in Columbus' fleet; behind the central cross is the ancient symbol of the Incas, who ruled Peru before the Spaniards conquered it, the rising sun (Plate IX, figure 2).

Almost all the American countries south of the United States were once subject to the Spanish throne, and, their loyalty centred on this, they remained in peaceful union. When, however, Napoleon expelled the Spanish king, their loyalty was shattered and they achieved their independence. They thus became a number of separate countries; only for short periods did some of them remain united, but soon wars broke out even between these.

Their common origin is shown in the similarity of their flags. Their National and Merchant Flags are mostly tricolours—their leaders were greatly influenced by the ideals of the French Revolution—some of which are alike except for distinguishing emblems on the central stripe. Many of their Ensigns, and some of their National Flags, bear emblems too complicated to describe and more ornate than those usual on the flags of Europe: they include local plants, animals, landscapes, and traditions, and also—in commemoration of their break from Spanish rule—an ancient emblem, the 'Cap of Liberty', worn in the days of ancient Rome by slaves who had gained their freedom.

Mexico, which forms the southern part of North America, was once called 'New Spain'; like Brazil, it was an Independent Empire before becoming a Republic. Its flag is a vertical tricolour resembling that of Italy, green, white, and red. The emblem on the white stripe of its National and Merchant Flag, Ensign, and President's Standard refers to a legend of the Aztecs, who ruled the country before the Spaniards came: it represents a brown eagle holding a green serpent in its beak (Plate IX, figure 3).

The isthmus between North and South America was once united in the Central American Confederation, whose colours were white and blue. The five countries between which it is now divided still keep those colours, though one of them has added red.

The Flag of Guatemala is thus a vertical tricolour, of two blue stripes separated by one white. The badge on the central stripe of the State Flag and Ensign includes a Central American bird, the Quetzal.

Honduras uses the horizontal tricolour of dark blue and white, but

1. Canada

2. Flag of the (Latin) Races

3. Mexico

4. Brazil

5. Panama

6. Chile

7. Uruguay

8. Cuba

Plate IX

distinguishes its National and State Flags by placing five blue stars on the central stripe: these symbolize the five countries which formerly belonged to the Central American Confederation. The badge on the Ensign is unusually complicated: its chief feature is a pyramid rising from the sea.

The badge of Belize (British Honduras) on the coast of Central America includes the tools used for felling mahogany for which the region is famous.

The National Flag and Ensign of El Salvador is a horizontal tricolour, white between blue, and bears a very complicated badge: in an equilateral triangle is a range of five mountains, representing five Central American

Guatemala

El Salvador

DIOS, UNION Y LIBERTAD

Nicaragua

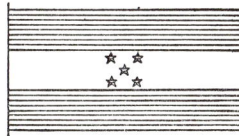

Honduras

volcanoes, over which is raised the Cap of Liberty. Another El Salvadorian flag bears the words 'Dios, Union y Libertad'.

The flag of Nicaragua is a horizontal tricolour, white between blue. The badge on the National and Merchant Flags and Ensign includes the triangle with the five mountains and the Cap of Liberty resembling those of El Salvador, but differs in its details.

The State Flag and Ensign of Costa Rica is not a tricolour, but is divided horizontally: dark-blue stripes along its top and bottom are separated by white stripes from a broader red stripe along its centre. On the red stripe is a badge depicting a landscape: three mountains, representing three volcanoes, separate two seas, representing the Pacific Ocean and the Caribbean Sea (between which the country lies). On each of the seas is a sailing ship. Above are seven stars representing the subdivisions of the country.

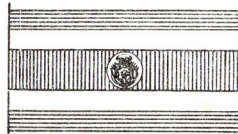

Costa Rica

Panama, which became an independent Republic only in the present century, has one simple but effective design which serves as Ensign, National Flag, and Merchant Flag. It is quartered: in the canton is a blue star, and in the fourth quarter a red star, both on white fields; the second quarter is red and the third blue (Plate IX, figure 5). It is appropriate that the country should fly these colours, for it is much influenced by the United States and hoists its flag on that country's Independence Day. The famous Panama Canal was constructed through American enterprise; the Canal Zone, five miles on either side, is under United States control and flies the Stars and Stripes.

The flag of the Governor of the Canal Zone is dark blue; on the white circle in its centre is a shield bearing a picture of a galleon passing between two adjoining coasts; above is a row of short vertical stripes, seven white and six red, and below the shield a scroll bears the words, 'The Land Divided, the World United'— by the Panama Canal.

Governor of the
Panama Canal Zone

The island of Puerto Rico, a self-governing Commonwealth of the United States in the Caribbean Sea, flies a flag which its people carried when, together with the people of Cuba, they rebelled against rule by Spain: five stripes alternately red and white, with a white star on a blue triangle in the hoist.

Some of the islands in the Caribbean Sea form independent Republics. Cuba remained a Spanish colony until liberated near the end of last century by the Spanish-American War. Perhaps because it was for a time under the protection of the United States of America, its flags are red, white, and blue, and bear stripes and a star. Its National and Merchant Flag and Ensign

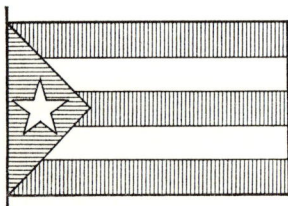

Puerto Rico

consists of five horizontal stripes, three blue and two white; in the hoist is a red triangle bearing one five-pointed white star representing the 'Star of Hope' and the blood of the patriots who fell in the cause of freedom (Plate IX, figure 8). The Jack places the white star in a red square in the canton; the rest of its upper half is white and its lower half is blue.

The Island of Haiti, once known as Hispaniola, now consists of two separate Republics. The Merchant Flag of its eastern part, the Dominican Republic, is a white cross of St. George's type, on a field of which the first and fourth quarters are blue and the second and third red; the red symbolizes the blood of the island's patriots, the blue the ideal of freedom, and the white the sacrifice they made for it. The National Flag and Ensign bears the country's arms at the centre of the white cross.

The western part of the island, the Republic of Haiti, was once ruled by France, and thus flew the tricolour of blue, white, and red. When it became an independent Negro Republic, its leader is said to have ripped away the central stripe from the French tricolour to show that the reign of the white man had ceased, leaving the blue to symbolize the negroes and the red the mulattos (of mixed blood). This was later changed to a flag divided horizontally, blue over red. In 1964, however, a new flag was adopted; it is halved vertically, black in the hoist and red in the fly. The State Flag and Ensign has a rectangle at the centre, showing the emblems of war grouped round a palm tree (the national coat of arms).

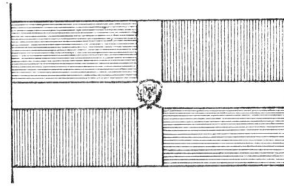

Dominican Republic

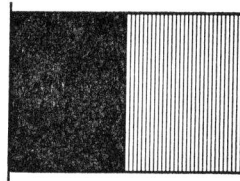

Haiti

The three countries in the north-west of South America at one time formed an independent Federal Union, Greater Colombia. Though they are now separate, they fly flags of similar colours distinguished by slight differences: horizontal tricolours of yellow, blue, and red.

On the National Flag of Colombia the yellow stripe occupying its upper half is twice the width of the dark-blue and red stripes. At the centre of the Merchant Flag is a blue, red-bordered oval containing a white star. The Ensign bears at its centre the complicated national badge, which includes a marine view and the Cap of Liberty.

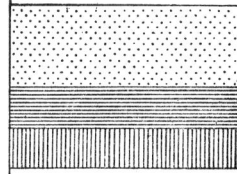

Colombia

Except for the proportions and shade of blue, the National and Merchant Flag of Ecuador is identical with the National Flag of Colombia, consisting of a yellow stripe twice as wide as the blue and red. The State Flag and Ensign bears at the centre the national arms the design of which includes a South American bird, the Condor, a snow-capped peak (Chimborazo, the highest mountain in

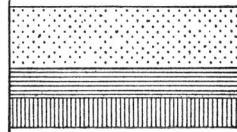

Ecuador

the country) with a steamship in the offing, and four Signs of the Zodiac.

The flags of Venezuela resemble the National Flag of Colombia, except

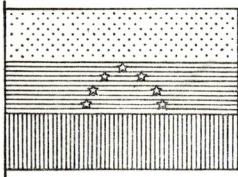

Venezuela

that the three stripes of yellow, blue, and red are equal in width. On the blue stripe are seven white stars, representing the country's original seven provinces. The State Flag and Ensign places the national arms in the hoist on the upper stripe.

The flags of the other countries of South America differ widely from each other not only in colour but also in design.

Guyana, formerly British Guiana, has adopted a new flag bearing a design of red and yellow triangles, separated by black and white edgings, and placed on a green background; the former badge displayed a full-rigged sailing ship at sea, and a scroll bearing the Latin motto, 'We Both Give and Seek'.

The National Flag of Peru is a vertical tricolour, two red stripes separated

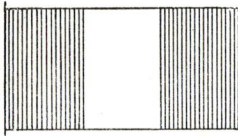

Peru

by white. The State Flag and Ensign includes the national arms on the white stripe: a shield bearing a South American animal, the llama, yellow on a blue field; a tree, green on a white field, and an ancient classical emblem, the 'Horn of Plenty', yellow on a red field. The Jack is square, with the national arms at the centre of a white field with a red border.

Bolivia is named after the leader who liberated South America from Spain, Simón Bolívar. Its National Flag is a horizontal tricolour of red, yellow, and green. The State Flag bears the national arms on the yellow stripe: a highly complicated design at the centre of which is the mountain of Potosí, rich in silver, a tree, a wheatsheaf, and an alpaca. These emblems and the colours of the flags represent the country's natural wealth in

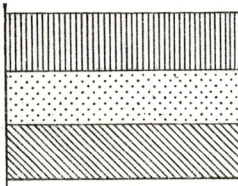

Bolivia

minerals (yellow), forests and crops (green), and animals (red).

The flag of Paraguay is a horizontal tricolour of red, white, and blue; on the white stripe, upon the obverse side, is a badge showing a gold star within a wreath of palm and olive; the device on the reverse includes a golden lion and the red Cap of Liberty.

Chile, occupying the coastal strip between the southern Andes and the sea, has broken away from the typical design of vertical or horizontal stripes. Its Flag is halved horizontally: in the canton is a blue square containing a five-pointed white star; the rest of the upper half is white and the lower half is red (Plate IX, figure 6).

The Merchant Flag of the Argentine Republic consists of a horizontal tricolour of two light-blue stripes separated by white. The State Flag and Ensign bears at the centre of the white stripe the emblem of the sun, represented as a human face surrounded by rays. The Jack is square and places the sun emblem at the centre of a white field with a blue border.

The Falkland Islands lie off the southern part of the Argentinian coast. Their badge, which appears on the Blue Ensign, shows a hornless ram on a blue field; on blue and white stripes representing the sea appears the ship *Desire* on which John Davies discovered the islands in 1592; below is the punning motto, 'Desire the Right'.

Uruguay, which before it became independent belonged at different times both to the Spanish Empire and to Brazil, has flags of a distinctive pattern. In the canton of its National and Merchant Flag and Ensign is a sun emblem,

Argentina

differing somewhat from that of the Argentine, yellow on a square white field; the field of the flag itself consists of five white and four blue stripes (Plate IX, figure 7). The Jack consists of three horizontal stripes, blue, white, and blue, with a red stripe diagonally across them.

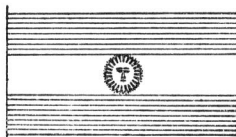

Brazil, largest and most easterly country in South America, was colonized from Portugal; even when it gained its independence it was for a time ruled by a Portuguese emperor. Though now a Republic, it still keeps the general design and the colours of its Imperial Flag, but has replaced its old coat of arms by a republican emblem. Its National and Merchant Flag and Ensign consists of a yellow diamond on a green field: the diamond encloses a blue circle, representing a globe, with a girdle on its equator bearing words meaning 'Order and Progress'; above the girdle is a large white star and below it are twenty-two smaller stars (Plate IX, figure 4).

A number of islands within or somewhat beyond the Caribbean form part of the British Commonwealth. Some of them place a special badge on the Blue Ensign, others have special flags. Some of these islands belong to the Greater Antilles, the Lesser Antilles consisting of the Leeward and Windward Islands.

A gold saltire divides the flag of Jamaica into four triangular segments: green above and below, and black in the hoist and fly. The Queen's Personal Flag places the Royal Emblem at the centre of a St. George's Cross with broad arms, on each of which is displayed a golden pineapple.

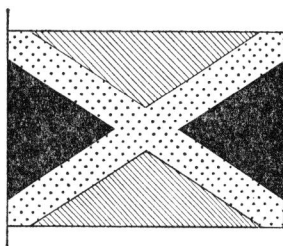

Jamaica

B.F.—6

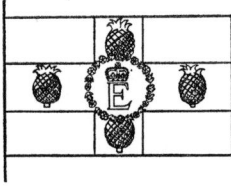

Jamaica
(Queen's Flag)

Trinidad and Tobago
(Queen's Flag)

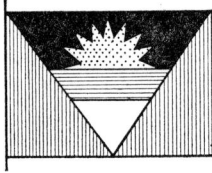

Antigua

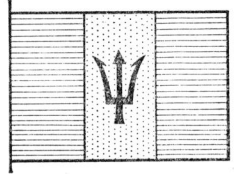

Barbados

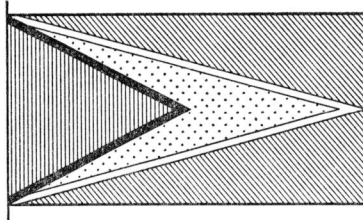

Guyana

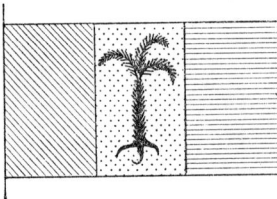

St. Christopher-Nevis

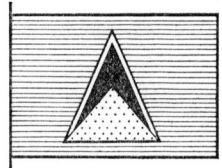

St. Lucia

Bahamas
(obsolete)

Bermuda

Dominica

Leeward Islands
(obsolete)

Montserrat

St. Vincent

Turks and Caicos
Islands

British Virgin Islands

Windward Islands
(obsolete)

Belize
(British Honduras)

Falkland Islands

Cayman Islands

Near Jamaica are the Cayman Islands. Their badge consists of their shield, displaying a lion, gold on red, above three green stars on three wavy blue and white bars representing the sea; and of their crest, a pineapple behind a tortoise; the motto reads, 'He Hath Founded It Upon the Seas'.

The group known as the Leeward Islands formerly used a badge showing two sailing ships and a large pineapple, in the foreground; above are the Royal Arms. In the group are Montserrat, whose badge displays a green-robed female figure clinging to a large cross with a harp at its foot. The badge of the British Virgin Islands represents a white-robed female figure holding an antique lamp; eleven similar lamps form two vertical rows. A scroll below bears the Latin word, *Vigilate* (Watch). The American Virgin Islands display the emblem of the United States, the eagle, in gold between the letters 'V' and 'I'.

The red flag of Antigua bears a large inverted triangle striped horizontally: black, displaying the rising sun in gold, blue, and white. The flag of St. Christopher-Nevis is a vertical tricolour, light green, yellow, and light blue, with the silhouette of a palm tree in black on the central stripe. Anguilla, however, prefers to use a flag displaying three orange dolphins above a light blue stripe on a white field.

The shield on the badge of the Windward Islands was quartered red,

Anguilla

yellow, green, and white; below it a scroll bore a Latin motto meaning, 'Go With a Fortunate Foot'. One of these islands, St. Vincent, uses a badge representing two female figures at an altar, one holding an olive-branch, the other kneeling as though offering sacrifice: the Latin motto means, 'Peace and Justice'; it now appears at the centre of a blue flag.

The badge of Dominica includes the island's full coat of arms: the shield is quartered and displays a coconut tree, a Dominican edible toad, a Carib canoe, and a banana tree; the crest is a lion, the supporters are parrots, and the motto could be translated 'After the Good Lord we love the soil'.

The flag of Grenada was until recently divided horizontally, blue, yellow, and green; with a nutmeg at its centre shown in natural colours on a white oval. That of St. Lucia is blue and bears a device of triangles, one yellow and the other black with a white border.

The National Flag of Barbados bears three vertical stripes, blue, gold, and blue; on its central stripe appears the head of a trident in black.

The red flag of Trinidad and Tobago, islands off the north coast of Venezuela, is crossed, from the top of the hoist to the bottom of the fly, by a diagonal black stripe fimbriated with white. The Queen's Personal

Flag places the Royal Emblem centrally on a flag displaying two humming-birds and the three ships of Christopher Columbus.

North of the Greater Antilles are the Bahamas, now the Commonwealth of the Bahamas. Formerly their flag was the Blue Ensign with their badge: three ships within a garter, surmounted by the Royal Crown and bearing a Latin motto meaning 'Pirates Expelled and Commerce Restored'. Their new National Flag is a horizontal tricolour, blue, yellow, and blue, with a black triangle in the hoist. The badge of the Turks and Caicos Islands shows three of the islands' products: a queen-conch shell, a spiny lobster and a Turk's head cactus.

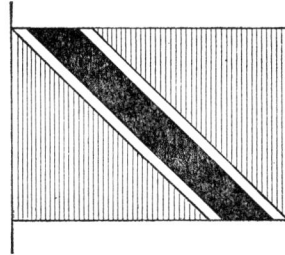

Trinidad and Tobago

Bermuda lies further out in the Atlantic off the east coast of the United States. The badge on its flag shows a shield displaying a red lion grasping another shield on which is represented the shipwreck of the *Sea Venture* in 1609; it appears on the Red Ensign.

11

THE FLAGS OF EUROPE

Lift up a standard for the people

THE BIBLE

As 'the shorthand of history', flags form part of the tradition of the nations which fly them. Peoples who are related, or who have had a similar history, are akin in ideals, and usually express them by flying the same type of flag. Similar flags do not, however, always mean similar ideals or history—two widely different nations may hit on the same flag-patterns by accident, or one may deliberately copy another.

The European people most akin to ourselves are the Scandinavians. Their languages show a resemblance to English and their ideals and traditions are very like ours; through our Viking ancestors they are actually related to us. It is not surprising, then, that their emblems are similar to that of England, the St. George's Cross. Their flags, however, differ from ours not only in colour but in small details. The vertical arm of their crosses is not in the mid-line of the flag but nearer to the hoist, they do not include any saltires (diagonal crosses), and there may be a third tongue in the middle of their swallow-tail flags. Their rulers may follow a custom not used in Britain: a ship may wear a special pendant to show that a member of the Royal Family is on board but does not wish to be treated with ceremony.

The emblem of Denmark is the exact reverse of that of England; a white cross on a red field. This is called the *Dannebrog*, the 'Strength of Denmark'; it is probably the oldest national flag still in use, the Danes having a tradition that it was revealed in a vision to King Waldemar on the field of battle over seven hundred years ago. The Merchant and National Flag is almost square, the Jack and Ensign is longer and ends in swallow-tails (Plate X, figure 1).

Norway was once ruled by the same king as Denmark, and its emblem is derived from the *Dannebrog*: the white cross on the red field, but with a narrower blue cross running along it. The National and Merchant Flag is oblong, the Jack is square; the Ensign and Government Flag is also swallow-tailed but with a central tongue (Plate X, figure 2).

Iceland, once ruled by the King of Norway, and more recently by the King of Denmark, is now an independent Republic. Still, however, it flies the Norwegian colours reversed: a red cross with a white border on a blue field (it thus resembles the first British Union Flag except that it has no white saltire). The National and Merchant Flag is rectangular, the Government Flag and Ensign is swallow-tailed (Plate X, figure 3).

74

1. Denmark

2. Norway

3. Iceland

4. Sweden

5. Finland

6. Greece

7. Czechoslovakia

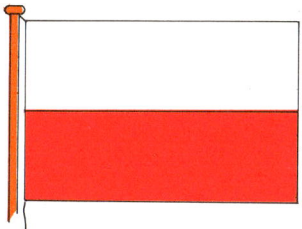

8. Poland

Plate X

The flag of the Faroe Islands bears a red cross, bordered with blue, on a white field.

Greenland, which like the Faroes is regarded as politically part of Denmark, flies the Danish flag. It is represented on the Royal Arms of Denmark by the symbol of a bear, the Faroe Islands by that of a ram.

The flag of Sweden, which is over four hundred years old, bears the colours of the Swedish Royal Family, a yellow cross on a light-blue field. The National and Merchant Flag has a square fly, the Ensign and Jack have swallow-tails with a central tongue (Plate X, figure 4).

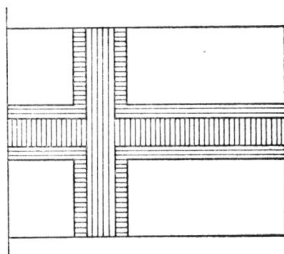

Faroe Islands

The national colours of Finland are light blue for its lakes and white for its snows. The National Flag consists of a blue cross with broad arms on a white field; the State Flag bears the National Arms on the centre of the cross; the Ensign is similar to the State Flag except that it has a swallow-tail with a central tongue (Plate X, figure 5).

The Åland Islands in the northern Baltic are part of Finland and their own flag is flown only on land. It unites the colours of Sweden and Finland, a red cross within a yellow cross on a blue field.

Outside Scandinavia, most European countries fly tricolour flags, either vertical or horizontal, and the majority of these flags conform to the heraldic rules by having a metal stripe (white or yellow) between two colours. Some of the countries, whose history has brought them into contact with ourselves, use the same colours as we do, red, white, and blue.

The tricolour of our nearest Continental neighbour, France, is comparatively recent. One of her oldest flags was the banner of St. Denis, the country's patron

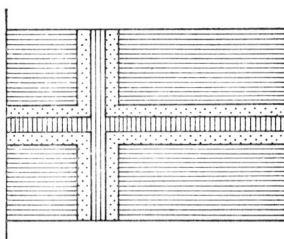

Åland Islands

saint; this, however, began to go out of use after the Battle of Agincourt. Called the *Oriflamme*, it was probably a red banner with its fly cut into tongues to resemble flames. The Royal Emblem of France at first consisted of golden toads—it is not surprising that this was altered to the golden lilies, the fleurs-de-lis. St. Joan's pendant, which led the French armies to victory, bore religious emblems in the hoist and the Royal Lilies in the fly.

The French Revolution swept the lilies away and introduced a tricolour, using a design perhaps suggested by an earlier revolutionary flag, that of the Netherlands. Napoleon devised an Imperial Standard bearing a design of golden bees; later, for a time, the French Monarchy brought back the lilies; but when France became once more a Republic it restored the tricolour.

The French National Flag, Merchant Flag and Ensign consists of a vertical tricolour, blue, white, and red; the stripes differ slightly in width, being so calculated as to appear exactly equal (Plate XI, figure 3). The President's flag is usually a square tricolour, with his initials, in gold, at its centre.

The flag of Belgium is also a vertical tricolour, and was originally a revolutionary flag. Its people, when they revolted against the former rulers, the Hapsburgs, rallied under the flag of Brabant (a region now divided between Holland and Belgium), and this revolt gave its name to the Belgian National Anthem, the *Brabançonne*, and its colours to the Belgian flag. The National and Merchant Flag is a tricolour of black, yellow, and red (Plate XI, figure 4).

The tricolour of the Netherlands—often called Holland—was originally orange, white, and blue. These were the colours of William, Prince of Orange, who freed the country from Spanish rule. This *Princevlag* is still sometimes flown, although—perhaps for greater distinction at sea—the orange stripe on the official flag has been changed to red (Plate XI, figure 5). The National and Merchant Flag and Ensign is thus a horizontal tricolour of red, white, and blue; the Jack consists of twelve triangles, three of each colour, with the points meeting at the centre.

The Grand Duchy of Luxembourg flies a horizontal tricolour rather like that of the Netherlands. It is, however, longer, and its colours, taken from the Duchy's coat of arms, are red, white, and *medium* blue.

Unlike the countries already mentioned, most of which have existed for hundreds of years, Germany became a Nation only during the last century; it was a union of a number of states varying in size and importance, each with its own colours and flag. The North German Confederation, formed in 1867, adopted the black and white of its leading state, Prussia, and the red and white of a great medieval trading corporation, the Hanseatic League. The first German National Flag was thus a horizontal tricolour of black, white, and red.

In 1871 Germany became an empire and the imperial flags with the black eagle were introduced, though the old flag was retained as the Merchant Flag.

At the end of the First World War the Empire fell and the country became a Republic. The new National Flag it adopted was also a tricolour, but its colours were black, red, and gold; the Merchant Flag, however, remained black, white, and red but bore the new colours in a small canton. The Nazi Government showed their dislike of the Republic by abolishing the flag: they restored the old tricolour of black, white, and red, flying it side by side with their own flag. Later they abolished even the old tricolour and flew

FLAGS OF EUROPE (2)

1. Union of Soviet Socialist Republics

2. Switzerland

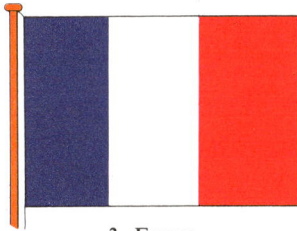

3. France

4. Belgium

5. Netherlands

6. Turkey

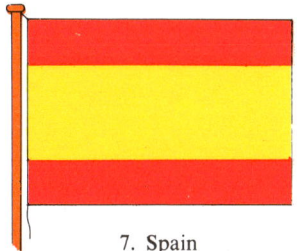

7. Spain

8. Portugal

Plate XI

only their own flag: a red flag with a large white circle at its centre containing an ancient magical sign, the black Swastika.

Germany now consists of two Independent Nations. The Federal Republic of (West) Germany has restored the former emblem, so that its horizontal tricolours are of black, red, and gold. The President's flag is gold with a red border, bearing a black eagle. The German Democratic Republic (East Germany) also uses the black, red, and gold tricolour, but distinguishes it by displaying a hammer and a pair of dividers encircled by a wreath of corn. The Head of State's Flag places this emblem on a red flag bordered on three sides by a black, red, and gold cord.

Federal Republic
of Germany

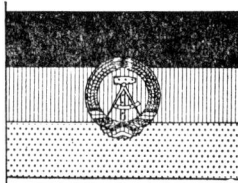

Like Germany, Italy did not become a united Nation until the middle of last century[1]; not only had it previously consisted of a number of small states, but much of the country had actually been under foreign rule, that of Austria. The new Kingdom of Italy adopted the flag devised by Napoleon when he had been ruler of Italy; it was similar to the French tricolour but with green instead of blue. The national arms were placed in the centre of this flag, and thus it remained until after World War II when Italy

German Democratic
Republic

became a Republic and the arms were removed, leaving the plain tricolour as the National Flag. Since Mexico had adopted a similar tricolour as its Merchant Ensign, the Merchant Flag of Italy was differenced by a shield, on its white stripe, containing the emblems of four of the historic republics which once flourished on the Italian coast. The Naval Ensign places a crown above this shield.

The traditional colours, white and red, of Malta, are said to have been those of Roger the Norman, who is reported to have landed on the island in 1090. The Maltese Traditional Flag remained unchanged until 1943, when, in token of the Island's heroic stand during the Second World War, King George VI authorized the George Cross to be displayed on a blue canton in the hoist, and also to be added to the shield on the Governor General's Standard. Since Malta became independent in 1964, the Cross has appeared in silver, direct on the white half. In 1965 the island adopted a Merchant Flag, showing the Maltese Cross in white at the centre of a red, white-bordered flag. The Personal Flag of Queen Elizabeth II for Malta

[1] Vatican City, though in Rome, is an independent State; as the Headquarters of the Roman Catholic Church it will be dealt with later in the chapter on International Flags.

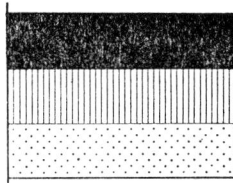

places the letter 'E' and the Royal Crown within a circle of roses upon the island's Traditional Flag.

Until it was forcibly merged into Germany, Austria had only one flag, a horizontal tricolour: two broad red stripes separated by white. These were the colours of the old Dukes of Austria, and are said to have been copied from the bloodstains on the white cloak which a twelfth-century Crusader had worn in battle. The flag went out of use during the German occupation of Austria, being replaced by the Nazi Swastika flag; now that Austria is again an independent Republic, its ancient tricolour has been restored.

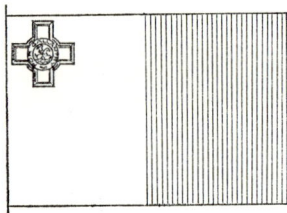

Traditional Flag of Malta, G.C.

The flag of Spain used to be a horizontal tricolour, red above and below and yellow between; these, the old colours of Aragon, are said to have been copied, rather like those of Austria, from the marks made by a king who dipped his fingers in blood and drew them over a yellow shield. When Spain became a Republic in 1931, the lower stripe was made purple instead of red, but when General Franco came to power he restored the former colours. The Merchant Flag is the plain tricolour of red, yellow, and red (Plate XI, figure 7); the State Flag and Ensign bear the National Arms on the central stripe: this includes the emblems of several of the old Spanish kingdoms and is flanked by two pillars representing the 'Pillars of Hercules' (Gibraltar and the African cape opposite). The design also includes a black eagle.

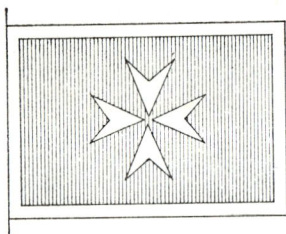

Malta, Merchant Flag

The badge of Gibraltar symbolizes its nature. On a red shield of unusual shape appears a three-towered castle, in natural colour, with battlements and arrow-slit windows; attached to its door is a gold key, and below is a scroll bearing Latin words meaning 'The Badge of Mount Calpe'. This is the ancient name of Gibraltar, which is both a stronghold and the 'key to the Mediterranean'. The people of 'The Rock' also fly an unofficial flag which displays the castle and key emblem on a white field with a broad red stripe along its lower edge.

Gibraltar

Although Portugal became a Republic in 1910, it still places on its flag a coat of arms similar to that of its former Royal Family. Its National Flag and Ensign is not a tricolour but is divided vertically with green in the hoist and red in the fly; the red is considerably wider than the green. On the dividing line is a yellow Armillary Sphere (a 'skeleton' sphere once used as an astronomical instrument—formerly part of the arms of Brazil, then a Portuguese Colony). In this are the national arms, a white shield bearing five small shields; it has a red border on which are seven yellow castles, and each small shield is blue and contains five white circles arranged saltire-fashion, celebrating a victory over five Moorish princes (Plate XI, figure 8). The Jack places the arms and sphere on the centre of a square flag, red with a green border.

Bordering on France are two tiny countries, each with its own flag. The Principality of Andorra, in the Pyrenees, combines in its emblem the colours of the countries to its north and south, the French red and blue and the Spanish red and yellow: its flag is a vertical tricolour of blue, yellow, and red, with a coat of arms on the central stripe. The Principality of Monaco, famous for the town of Monte Carlo, flies a flag divided horizontally, red above white; the State Flag bears on a white field the arms of the Grimaldi family, from which its Prince is descended.

The National and the Merchant Flags of Switzerland both bear the same emblem. This is unlike that of any other country because of the Republic's unique history: it was founded in the fourteenth century by a union of peasants who had successfully revolted against their oppressive rulers. Its founders regarded their fight for freedom as a cause as sacred as the Crusades and therefore chose as their emblem a white Greek Cross (a cross with equal arms) on a red field (Plate XI, figure 2).

The National Flag of Poland is halved horizontally, white above red. The Ensign is similar but has swallow-tails (Plate X, figure 8). The Jack places the National Emblem, a white eagle on a red shield, on a red-bordered white flag. The President's Flag displays the eagle on a red flag with an ornamental border.

Most of the countries in south-eastern Europe have a custom not found elsewhere, that of decorating their Presidential Standards with a border of tiny triangles in the national colours.

Czechoslovakia was formed after the 1914 War in order to restore the independence of some historic states, whose colours appear in its flag: the red and white of Bohemia and the blue of Moravia. As so many other nations fly these colours, however, the new state adopted an original design: its National Flag is halved horizontally, white above red, except for a blue triangle in the hoist (Plate X, figure 7).

Yugoslavia, also formed after the 1914 War, was formerly called the Kingdom of the Serbs, Croats, and Slovenes, but it is no longer a Monarchy. Its State and Merchant Flags are horizontal tricolours of blue, white, and red and bear a large red star bordered with yellow. A similar design forms

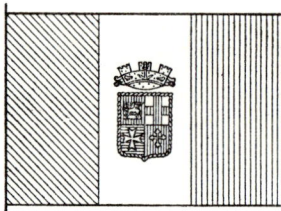

Italy

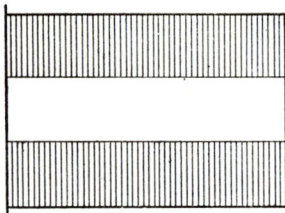

Austria

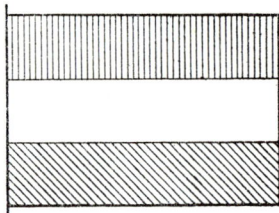

Hungary

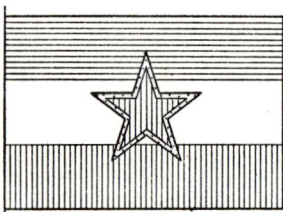

Yugoslavia

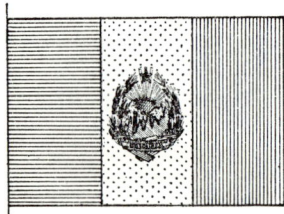

Rumania

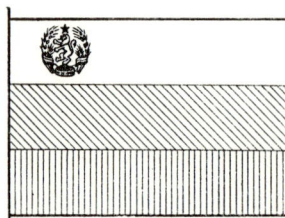

Bulgaria

Albania

the canton of the Ensign, the field of which is red. The States of Serbia and Montenegro, Croatia, and Slovenia, also fly tricolours, respectively red, blue, and white; red, white, and blue; white, blue, and red; each bears a star.

The National Flag, Merchant Flag, and Ensign of Hungary also consists of a horizontal tricolour, but of red, white, and green.

The flag of Rumania is a vertical tricolour of blue, yellow, and red, said to represent the sky, the wealth of the country's soil and the courage of its people; the national coat of arms appears on the yellow stripe.

The National and Merchant Flags of Bulgaria are horizontal tricolours of white, green, and red; in the former on the white stripe, in the hoist, is the emblem of the State. The Ensign is white, with two horizontal stripes, green above red, along its lower edge; in the upper hoist is a large red star.

The Merchant Flag of Albania is a horizontal tricolour, black between two red stripes; on the black stripe is a red star with a gold fimbriation. Its National Flag bears a black double-headed eagle on a red field; this formed the arms of the great fifteenth-century patriot Scanderberg: above this is a red star edged with yellow.

The National and State Flags of Greece are striped horizontally, blue and white; a square in the canton displays a Greek (equal-armed) Cross, white on blue (Plate X, figure 6). The State Flag places a golden crown in the centre of the cross. A simpler flag, the white cross on the blue field, was formerly flown inland. The Cross commemorates the resistance which Greece made for centuries in defence of Christianity against the Moslems.

The flag of Cyprus displays a map of the island, in gold, above two crossed olive-branches, in green, on a white field.

Turkey, as the Ottoman Empire, was once master of the Balkans and dominated the Mediterranean; today it consists of Asia Minor, and of a small region in Europe bordering on the Bosporus. Its National and Merchant Flag, Ensign and Jack still displays the emblem which was once the terror of the sea: a crescent moon and a star on a red field (Plate XI, figure 6). The crescent is the ancient symbol of Byzantium: the story goes that when Philip of Macedonia, father of Alexander the Great, was trying to storm it by a surprise night attack, the moonlight revealed his scheme; the city

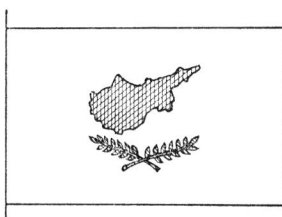

Cyprus

retained this emblem not only when it was Christianized and renamed Constantinople, but when it was conquered by the Turks—who now call it Istanbul. Its field was for a time changed to the Mohammedan sacred colour, green, but later the traditional red colour was restored.

Russia was until 1917 an Empire; its Merchant Flag was then a horizontal tricolour of white, blue, and red, and its Ensign a blue saltire on a white field. The Imperial Standard of the Czar bore a double-headed eagle, black on a yellow field, a device which dates from the Byzantine Empire of the fifteenth century.

The Imperial Government was autocratic, but among the political groups which met in secret was the Communist Party, whose emblem was the red flag. This is a symbol on which very different opinions are held: its enemies accuse it of meaning bloodshed and destruction, its supporters hail it as signifying the blood-brotherhood of all mankind. It has long been the flag of revolution the world over.

After the fall of the Imperial Government the Communists, headed by Lenin and Trotsky, assumed control of Russia. They renamed the country the Union of Soviet Socialist Republics, and they needed a new flag as its emblem. It was only natural that they should choose the flag under which they had made their plans and dared arrest.

The State and Merchant Flag of the U.S.S.R. has at the top of the hoist the crossed hammer and sickle, the emblem of the workers in town and country; above this is a five-pointed star, an ancient symbol of authority: these are yellow on a red field (Plate XI, figure 1). The Ensign is white, with a blue stripe along its lower edge: the emblems appear in red, the star in the hoist and the hammer and sickle in the fly. The Jack is red and bears a red star with a white edging; on the red star, also in white, are the crossed hammer and sickle.

The various Soviet Republics which constitute the Union have red flags which bear the National Emblem, the crossed hammer and sickle, near the top of the hoist. They are distinguished from the State Flag of the U.S.S.R. by stripes of various colours.

Small U.S.S.R. flags were scattered on the surface of the moon by the first space rocket to reach it: the Russian *Lunik II*, launched in 1959; and the first unmanned space craft *Luna 9*, which landed on the moon in February 1966, carried red pennants bearing the Soviet coat of arms and the words 'Union of Soviet Socialist Republics', written in the Cyrillic alphabet. In 1972 pennants showing a relief of Lenin and the State Emblem of the U.S.S.R. were carried to Venus.

Pennant carried to the moon by *Luna 9*

12

THE FLAGS OF ASIA

Every man of the children of Israel shall pitch by his
own standard, with the ensign of their father's house.

THE BIBLE

THE countries of Asia and Africa cover so vast an area that they have never shared, like those of Europe, in one great civilization, with a common tradition and ideals. Their flags are very dissimilar: they include strange emblems, produced by ways of thought which we find hard to understand.

In the Near East, however, are a number of regions developed from the great Islamic civilization which once stretched almost round the Mediterranean. Here most of the flags display one or both of the Islamic emblems, the crescent moon and star, or its colours, red, white, green, and black.

Turkey-in-Asia shares the flag of European Turkey, the crescent and star, white on a red field (Plate XI, figure 6). Syria, south of Turkey, flies a horizontal tricolour, red, white, and black, and now places an eagle on the central stripe instead of the former stars. The Hashemite Kingdom of the Jordan, formerly known as Transjordan, uses a flag striped horizontally black, white, and green; a red triangle in the hoist bears a white star. The Iraqi Democratic People's Republic—formerly called Iraq, and in earlier times known as Mesopotamia, the land 'between the rivers' (Euphrates and Tigris)—places three green stars on the central stripe of a horizontal tricolour, red, white, and black, like the former flag of Syria but shorter.

The flag of Kuwait, at the head of the Persian Gulf, is striped horizontally, green, white, and red, with a black trapezium in the hoist. Yemen, at the southern end of the Red Sea, adopted a horizontal tricolour, red, white, and black, resembling that of the United Arab Republic of which it once formed part, but bearing only one green star on the central stripe. In 1967, a number of states in the extreme south-west of the Arabian Peninsula were united as the People's Democratic Republic of Yemen; its flag consists of three horizontal stripes, red, white, and black, with a light-blue triangle displaying a red star in the hoist.

Though so different from the flags of the other Moslem countries, that of Saudi Arabia has a more definite religious meaning. Its green field bears, in white Arabic characters, the Moslem declaration

Saudi Arabia

83

of faith: 'There is no god but God, and Mohammed is the prophet of God'. Beneath this the National Flag displays a scimitar. The Ensigns display white anchors. The Merchant Ensign is unique in that it is triangular; in addition to the anchor it shows two crossed swords but has no inscription.

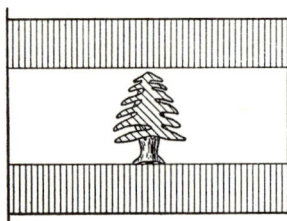

Lebanon

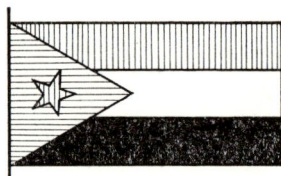

People's Democratic Republic of Yemen

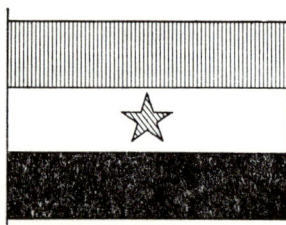

Yemen

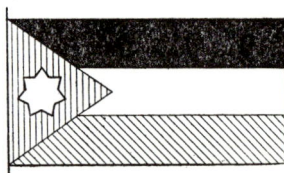

Jordan

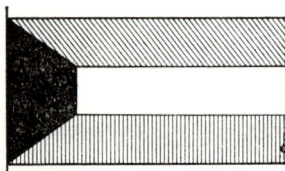

Kuwait

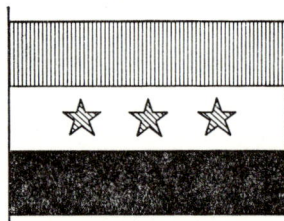

Iraqi Democratic People's Republic

On the Arabian shore of the Persian Gulf are several regions which were formerly under British protection. Bahrain, a group of islands half-way along the Gulf, uses a red flag; in the hoist is a broad white stripe whose edge may be either serrated or plain.

In striking contrast with the Islamic emblems are the flags of two nations on the eastern coast of the Mediterranean. That of Lebanon is a horizontal tricolour whose central white stripe is twice the width of the red stripe above and below. On this white stripe appears a cedar tree with green foliage and a brown trunk, recalling the 'Cedars of Lebanon' of which Solomon's temple was built.

Formerly under a British Mandate from the League of Nations and then

known as Palestine, the Jewish State of Israel became independent in 1948.
Its white flag bears two horizontal blue
stripes; between them, also in blue, is an
ancient religious emblem, the two interlaced
triangles forming the 'Shield of David'
(Plate XII, figure 1). The colours were suggested years ago by one of the founders of
Zionism, the ideal that this land should
again become, as in Biblical days, the
national home of the Jews: the blue represents the sky above Palestine, the white the
purity of the Zionist ideal. The Merchant
Flag places the interlaced triangles on a
white oval in the hoist of a blue flag.

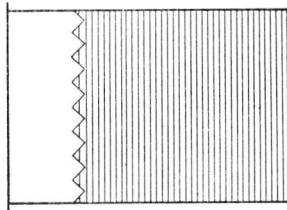

Bahrain

Iran, until 1935 called Persia, once used
a unique combination of colours: apple-
green, white, and pink. Its National and
Merchant Flag is now a horizontal tricolour of green, white, and red. In the
centre of the Government Flag is the
national emblem in yellow: the sun rising
over a lion which grasps a scimitar; in
that of the Military Flag and Ensign the
emblem is surrounded by a wreath over
which is a crown.

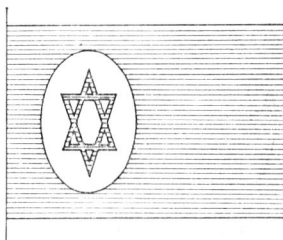

Merchant Flag of Israel

The National Flag of Afghanistan is a vertical tricolour of black, red,
and green—again the Islamic colours. The white appears on the red stripe
as the representation of a
mosque, between two flags,
within a wreath.

The Maldive Islands, off the
coast of India, fly a green red-
bordered flag, displaying the
Islamic crescent in white.

India formerly consisted of
what are now India, Pakistan,

Iran

and Bangladesh. Its flag was then the Blue Ensign with the 'Star of India'
in the fly: a five-pointed star surrounded by a blue heraldic 'garter', bearing
the words 'Heaven's Light Our Guide', surrounded by a circle of golden
rays.

In 1947 the country was divided into two. India, now a self-governing
Republic within the Commonwealth, consists only of those regions in which
most of the people are of the Hindu religion; those parts in which most are
Muslim became the Dominion of Pakistan.

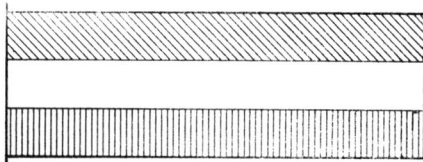

B.F.—7

The flag of India is a horizontal tricolour, saffron, white, and green; these colours represent courage, truth, and faith. On the central white stripe, in

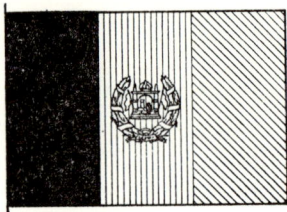

Afghanistan

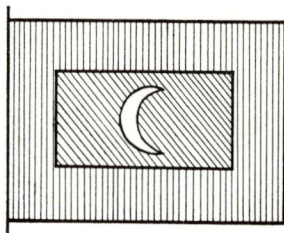

Maldive Islands

blue, is the symbol of India's ancient culture, the Wheel of Asoka—a great King of Northern India in the third century B.C. (Plate XII, figure 2). The Indian Navy's Ensign is white bearing a St. George's Cross broader than that on the White Ensign; in its canton is the Indian National Flag. This also appears in the canton of the Red Ensign of the Indian Merchant Navy.

'Star of India'

Bhutan, an independent State in the Himalayas, is subject to Indian guidance. Its flag is halved diagonally, orange-yellow in the hoist and red in the fly, and displays a wingless dragon in white.

The flag of the Dominion of Pakistan was a white crescent and star on a green field, with a broad white stripe down the hoist. This is the traditional emblem and colour of the Moslem faith; the white stripe represented those people of the Dominion who did not belong to that religion (Plate XII, figure 3). In 1971 the country divided into two regions, but the former West Pakistan, now Pakistan, which has withdrawn from the Commonwealth, retains the above emblem.

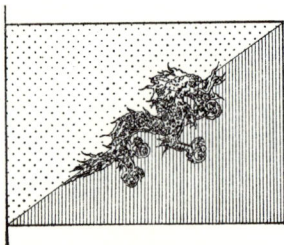

Bhutan

The former East Pakistan, now Bangladesh, remains within the Commonwealth. Its flag consists of a red disc at the centre of a green field. The disc originally bore a gold silhouette map of the region but this has been removed.

In early 1948 Ceylon, now called Sri Lanka, became a separate, self-governing Dominion within the Commonwealth and hoisted a flag displaying an ancient device of the Kings of Kandy: a lion brandishing a sword, representing the King as ruler of the State and commander of its armed forces. This country formerly flew the Blue Ensign with its badge in the fly:

a brown elephant standing on a patch of green in front of a grey pagoda, surrounded by a red circle containing gold ornaments. On the new flag the lion appeared, in gold, on a maroon background framed in a gold border to symbolize the protection of the nation by Buddhism. Two vertical bars, in the hoist, green and saffron, representing the Muslims and the Hindu Tamils, were added later. The present flag is shown on Plate XII, figure 4.

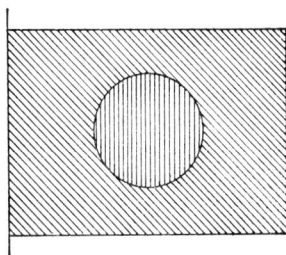

Bangladesh

Nepal, north-east of India, has a flag unique in shape, consisting of two right-angled triangles one above the other. It is crimson with a blue border, and bears two devices in white: that on the upper triangle represents the moon and that on the lower the sun.

Tibet, now occupied by the People's Republic of China, used to be ruled by the Dalai Lama, a Buddhist religious leader. The design of its former flag was striking: a large golden sun emitting blue and red rays. In the lower part of the flag a white triangle represented a snow-covered mountain—probably Mount Everest—over which the sun rises; at its foot were two lion-like beasts, white with green hair and tails, separated by religious symbols.

Former Badge of Ceylon

In 1947 Burma decided to leave the British Commonwealth of Nations and become an independent country. Formerly it had flown the Blue Ensign with its National Emblem in the fly: a peacock all proper on a gold field. Its National Flag is now red with a canton of dark blue. In the canton is a five

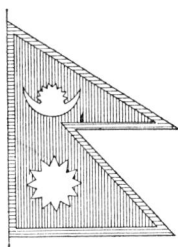

Nepal

Tibet

pointed large white star with five smaller white stars between the points. The red represents courage, the blue peace, and the white purity and honour;

the five stars represent the five races who form the people of Burma (Plate XII, figure 5). The Ensign bears the emblem in the canton of a white flag with a red cross of St. George type. The Merchant Flag is halved blue over red, with the stars in the hoist.

The Mongolian People's Republic, now independent of China, flies a vertical tricolour, red, blue, and red. In the hoist is the State Emblem, an ancient mystical sign, beneath a gold five-pointed star.

The ancient civilization of China was formerly ruled by an Emperor, whose flag bore a dragon on a yellow field (in Chinese legend the dragon is not a fearsome monster but a wise and benevolent friend). When the country became a Republic it adopted new flags: five horizontal stripes of red, yellow, blue, white, and black was the best known.

The island of Taiwan (Formosa) is still, at the time of writing, using the flag which it formerly used as Nationalist China, although the Government of the island has now no effective control over China as a whole. In the blue canton of its flags appears a white sun—the field of the National Flag is red, but that of the Merchant Flag is crossed by four yellow zigzag lines.

Taiwan

The National and Merchant Flag of the People's Republic of China is red, and bears in the canton a large five-pointed star in gold, with four smaller five-pointed stars arranged in a curve (Plate XII, figure 8).

The badge of Hong Kong, off the coast of China, consists of a white shield on which a naval crown appears above two junks on an heraldic sea. The crest is a crowned lion grasping a pearl and the supporters are a lion and a dragon.

Hong Kong

The flag of North Korea is a horizontal tricolour, consisting of a broad red stripe fimbriated in white between two narrow blue stripes. On the red stripe is a white circle containing a red star.

The flag of South Korea is white, and bears at its centre an ancient mystical emblem. This consists of a circle, divided by a curved line into halves of equal shape, coloured red and blue. In each of the corners is a group of three black parallel lines, broken and unbroken, which also have a mystical significance.

Japan proclaims itself the 'Land of the Rising Sun' and places this emblem on its flags. The National and Merchant Flag and Jack represents it as a red circle in the centre of a white field. The design of the Ensign is more striking, the sun, which is on the hoist side of the centre, being shown with sixteen red rays (Plate XII, figure 7). The Royal Standard

FLAGS OF ASIA

1. Israel

2. India

3. Pakistan

4. Sri Lanka

5. Burma

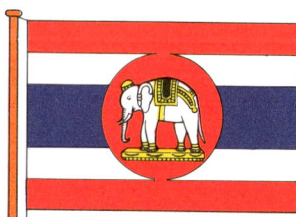

6. Thailand Ensign

7. Japan Ensign

8. People's Republic of China

Plate XII

bears the Emblem of the Imperial Family, the Chrysanthemum, gold on a red field.

Thailand, sometimes called Muang-thai or Siam, is the 'Country of the White Elephant', a sacred animal regarded almost as a patron saint. This emblem does not, however, appear on the country's National and Merchant Flag, which consists of five horizontal stripes: red along the top and bottom edges of the flags, with white separating them from the central stripe, which is blue and of double width. The Jack uses these stripes as a field to a golden anchor below a crown of Siamese pattern. The Ensign has on the centre of the stripes a red circle enclosing the sacred White Elephant (Plate XII, figure 6).

Indo-China includes four countries. What was formerly Cambodia is now the Khmer Republic and has adopted a new emblem. Its National Flag is medium blue with three white stars in the upper fly; the canton is red and contains a stylized emblem representing the temple, now in ruins, of Angkor Wat. Most of the territory, however, still flies the old Kingdom of Cambodia flag. The Republic of South Viet-Nam ('the Viet Cong') has a yellow star on a flag of red over light blue stripes. The red field and yellow star are the flag of the Democratic Republic of Viet-Nam. The flag of the Republic of Viet-Nam bears three narrow stripes, horizontal, in red on a yellow field. That of Laos bears on a red field the national emblem, a white three-headed elephant below a parasol. The Communists in Laos live under a horizontally striped flag of red-blue-red with a central white disc.

The regions in the southern part of the Malay Peninsula are members of the Commonwealth. Malaysia consists of the former Federation of Malaya, and of part of North Borneo. Until 1965 it also included the Island of Singapore. Its National Flag bears fourteen horizontal stripes, alternately red and white; its blue canton displays, in gold, a crescent and a fourteen-pointed

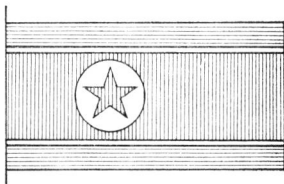

North Korea

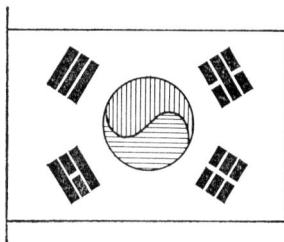

South Korea

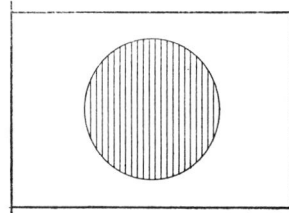

Japan

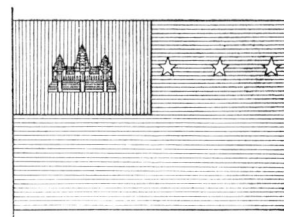

Khmer Republic

star, each stripe and each point of the star representing one of the fourteen States originally in the Federation. The colours include the royal

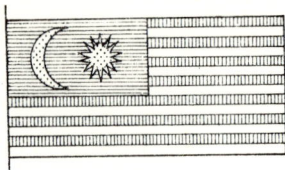

Malaysia

hue, gold, of the Malayan Sultans; in this region Islam is predominant, hence the crescent and star.

The crescent and star appear in white in the red canton of the blue flag of Johore; at the centre of the black white-bordered flag of Trengganu; and at the centre of the red flag of Kelantan, but here the crescent has its points upturned and the star is flanked by two lances and two swords. The emblem appears in white in the first quarter of the flag of Selangor, which is quartered red and yellow; and in gold in the blue canton of that of Malacca, the rest of the flag's upper half being red and its lower half white. In the upper hoist of the red flag of Kedah the crescent is green, and the star is replaced by a golden shield, the whole emblem being flanked by a golden wreath.

The flag of Penang is a vertical tricolour, light blue, white, and yellow,

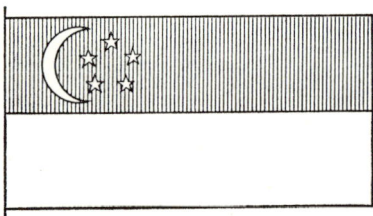

Singapore

Penang

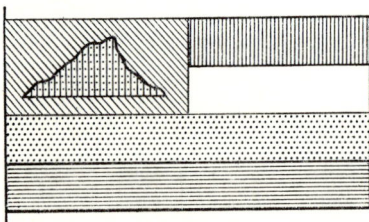

Sabah

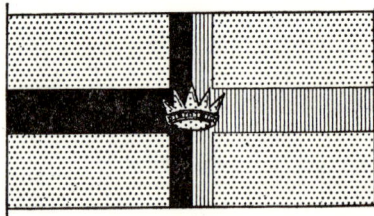

Sarawak

and displays a palm tree on the central stripe. The canton of the yellow flag of Negri Sembilan is halved diagonally, red and black. Two flags are halved horizontally, Perlis yellow and blue, and Pahang white and black; that of Perak is a horizontal tricolour, white, yellow, and black.

The flag of Sabah, formerly called British North Borneo, is striped horizontally, red, white, yellow, and blue; in the green canton a brown emblem represents Mount Kinabalu, the highest mountain in South-East Asia. Sarawak, also in the northern part of Borneo, still uses a flag bearing a design which the country's former Governor, Sir James Brooke—Rajah Brooke of Sarawak—based on his own personal arms. On a yellow field a cross of the St. George type is halved vertically, black in the hoist and red in the fly; at the centre of the cross appears a gold crown.

The island of Singapore, formerly united with Malaysia, became independent of the Federation in 1965. Its flag is halved horizontally, red above white, and displays the crescent and five stars in white in the upper hoist. This emblem, in white, appears in the red canton of the Ensign; the field is blue, with a large eight-pointed red and white star in the fly. The Merchant Flag is red and bears the crescent and stars emblem, with the stars uppermost, surrounded by a circle, all in white.

Although also situated in North Borneo, between Sabah and Sarawak, Brunei does not at present form part of Malaysia. Its yellow flag is crossed by a broad diagonal stripe, white above black. At its centre is the country's badge, showing in red a winged pylon within a crescent with upturned points flanked by two upraised arms; the motto means 'Always Render Service by God's Guidance'.

When in 1949 the Republic of the United States of Indonesia became independent of the Netherlands, it adopted the colours of its Nationalist Movement. Its flag is similar to that of Monaco, and to that of Poland reversed: it is halved horizontally, red above white.

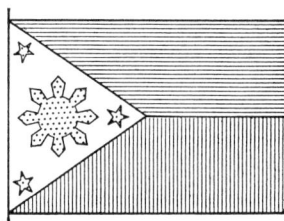

The Philippine Islands, formerly under United States protection, are

Brunei   Philippine Islands

now independent. Their flag is halved horizontally, blue above red, except for a white triangle in the hoist containing symbols, in yellow, of the sun and three stars.

13

THE FLAGS OF AFRICA

Every man in his place by their standards

THE BIBLE

LIKE most of the countries in the Near East, those in the northern part of Africa show that they originated in the great Islamic civilization. Some place on their flags the crescent and star, others use patterns of red, white, green, and black.

Egypt, until 1914, formed part of the Turkish Empire. As the United Arab Republic it adopted a horizontal tricolour, red, white, and black, with two five-pointed green stars on the central stripe (Plate XIII, figure 2). The country retained this flag when it became known as the Arab Republic of Egypt; later a gold hawk was substituted for the stars. Egypt has now entered into an alliance with Libya and the two countries may adopt new flags.

When under the guardianship of Egypt and Britain, the Sudan flew the flags of both these countries. Now an independent Republic, in 1970 it adopted a horizontal tricolour, red, white, and black, with a green triangle in the hoist. The present flag of Libya is like that of Egypt but is of larger proportions.

Until it gained its independence in 1962 the northern part of Algeria was part of 'Metropolitan France' and flew the French tricolour. The whole country now places the crescent and star, in red, at the centre of a flag divided vertically, green in the hoist and white in the fly (Plate XIII, figure 1). Only the star appears on the red flag of Morocco; it is outlined in green to form an ancient magical symbol, the pentagram. The green flag of Mauritania displays, in gold, the crescent moon with its points uppermost and the star above. The red flag of Tunisia displays the crescent and star, also in red, on a central white circle.

Further south many flags show the influence of France, which colonized much of this part of Africa. Two nations fly vertical tricolours of green, yellow, and red: that of Senegal is distinguished by a central green star; the tricolour of Mali formerly displayed a native dancer. Guinea uses the same colours but reverses them, its vertical tricolour being red, yellow, and green; Dahomey arranges the colours differently, with a

Morocco

broad green stripe down the hoist, and the fly divided horizontally, yellow over red. Of the other vertical tricolours that of Chad is blue, yellow , and red; that of the Ivory Coast is orange, white, and green and that of the Cameroun Republic, the French Cameroons until 1960, is green, red, and yellow, with two gold stars in the upper hoist.

Three countries use horizontal tricolours: Niger orange, white, and green, with a small orange circle at its centre; Upper Volta black, white, and red; and Gabon green, yellow, and blue.

Although members of the Commonwealth, four regions in West Africa also use tricolours. The horizontal stripes on that of The Gambia are red, blue, and green, separated by white fimbriations. On that of Sierra Leone the stripes, also horizontal, are green, white, and light blue; the Personal Flag of Queen Elizabeth II for Sierra Leone placed the Royal Emblem on a field symbolizing the country's name: the heraldic lion over the mountains (sierras).

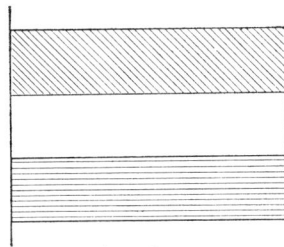

Sierra Leone

The independent Republic of Ghana uses a horizontal tricolour of red, gold (formerly white), and green; at its centre is a large black star, the emblem of freedom for the Africans.

The flag of the Federal Republic of Nigeria bears three vertical stripes, green, white, and green.

The distinctive emblem of Liberia symbolizes the country's origin: it was formed by an American society whose aim was to enable freed Negro slaves to form self-governing communities in their own land. Its National and Merchant Flag and Ensign therefore resembles the Stars and Stripes but has eleven red and white stripes to represent the eleven men who signed the country's Declaration of Independence in 1847; the one white star in

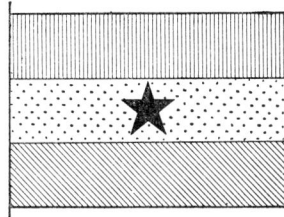

Ghana

the blue canton signifies that Liberia, unlike the U.S.A., is a unitary state (Plate XIII, figure 3).

Two other emblems, though not tricolours, are striped horizontally. The flag of Togo bears five horizontal stripes, alternately green and yellow; in the red canton is a white star. The four horizontal stripes, blue, white, green, and yellow, on the flag of the Central African Republic are crossed by a red vertical stripe, and there is a gold star in the upper hoist.

In contrast to these comparatively recently formed States, Ethiopia (formerly called Abyssinia) is about three thousand years old. Its flag is a horizontal tricolour, green, yellow, and red; these colours are said to

7*

represent the country's three regions and also to resemble the rainbow, which is often visible there. On the centre of the State Flag appears the crowned Lion of Judah.

In the extreme east of Africa is the Somali Democratic Republic, formed

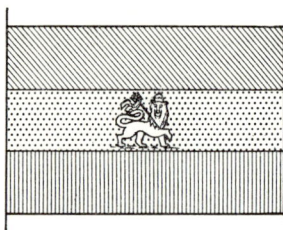

Ethiopia

Somalia

by the union of the former British Somaliland and Italian Somaliland. Though now independent, Somalia still uses the flag of the second of these territories, a white five-pointed star on a light-blue field.

Until 1972 the name 'Congo' was used to denote two distinct countries: these are now known as the People's Republic of the Congo and the Republic of Zaïre. The flag of the former is red; in the upper hoist it displays the emblem of a star above a crossed hammer and hoe in gold flanked by a green wreath. The Republic of Zaïre has a green flag, with the emblem of a brown arm, its hand grasping a brown torch with red flames, upon a gold disc.

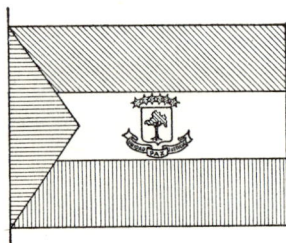

Equatorial Guinea

The State Flag of Equatorial Guinea is striped horizontally, green, white, and red. There is a blue triangle in the hoist, and a silver shield at its centre displays a native tree; above appear six gold stars and below is a motto, in Spanish, meaning 'Unity, Peace, Justice'. The National Flag omits the arms.

The vertical tricolour of Rwanda is red, yellow, and green, but is distinguished from that of Guinea by the letter 'R' on its central stripe. A white saltire divides the flag of Burundi into four triangles, red above and below, and green in the hoist and fly; on a central white circle are shown three green-bordered red stars.

Much of south central Africa consists of regions which are within the Commonwealth.

The flag of Uganda bears six horizontal stripes, black, yellow, and red; a crested crane is displayed on a small white circle at its centre (Plate XIII,

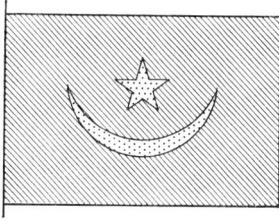

Mauritania

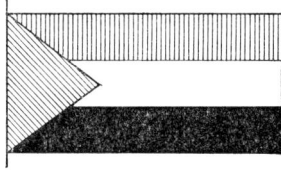

Sudan

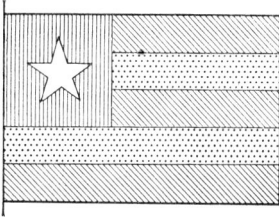

Togo

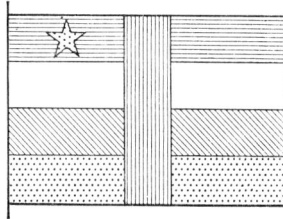

Central African Republic

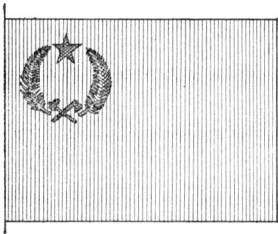

People's Republic of
the Congo

Republic of Zaïre

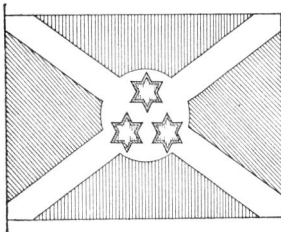

Burundi

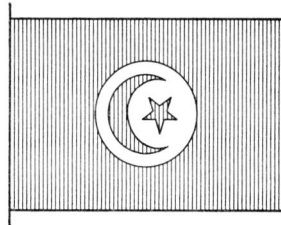

Tunisia

figure 5). That of Kenya is a horizontal tricolour, black, red fimbriated with white, and green; at its centre is an emblem of native weapons (Plate XIII, figure 4). That of Tanzania is green in the hoist and blue in the fly, and is crossed by a broad black diagonal stripe edged with gold (Plate XIII, figure 7).

Also included in the Commonwealth are two islands in the Indian Ocean. The badge of Seychelles shows a sea-beach below a blue sky; on the beach a palm tree is growing and a turtle is basking; the motto is Latin for

Seychelles

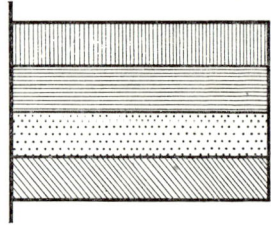

Mauritius

'The Finish Crowns the Work'. When Mauritius achieved independence within the Commonwealth it adopted a flag bearing four horizontal stripes, red, navy blue, yellow, and green.

The Federation of Rhodesia and Nyasaland was formed in 1953. It placed in the fly of the Blue Ensign the shield from its coat of arms; this included emblems from the badges of each of the three regions which formed it: the rising sun from the former shield of Nyasaland, the lion from that of Southern Rhodesia, and the vertical black and white wavy lines, representing the waters of Victoria Falls, from that of Northern Rhodesia. At the end of 1963, however, the Federation was dissolved, each of the regions adopting its own flag.

The flag of Zambia (formerly Northern Rhodesia) is green; in the upper part of the fly appears an orange-coloured eagle with outspread wings; below are three vertical stripes, red, black, and orange.

The horizontal tricolour of Malawi (formerly Nyasaland) is black, red, and green. At the centre of the black stripe appears a rising sun in red.

Rhodesia (formerly Southern Rhodesia) for a time flew a British ensign of light blue; the design in its fly was taken from the shield of the Rhodes

family: a red lion flanked by two thistles in green and purple appeared on a white field; below this a golden pick, an emblem of mining, was displayed on a green field. In 1968 it adopted a new flag divided vertically, green, white, and green; on the central stripe appears the Rhodesian coat of arms; the crest is the Great Zimbabwe Bird and the supporters are sable antelopes; the motto means 'May It be Worthy of the Name'.

Rhodesia   This new emblem symbolizes the Unilateral Declaration

Sierra Leone—Queen's Flag
(obsolete)

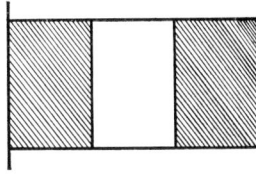

Nigeria

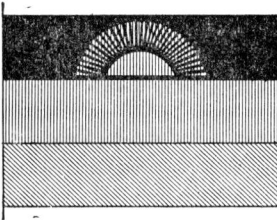

Malawi

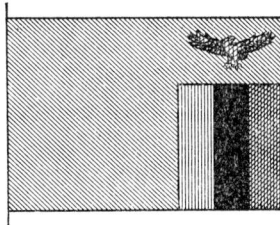

Zambia

Rhodesia

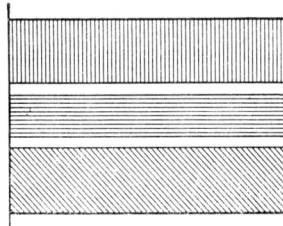

The Gambia

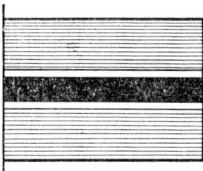

Botswana

Lesotho

of Independence made by Rhodesia in 1965; this has, however, not so far been recognized by Britain.

The Island of Madagascar, off the East Coast of Africa, was formerly a French Colony. It gained its independence in 1958 and, as the Malagasy Republic, now flies a flag bearing a broad white stripe down the hoist, the fly being halved horizontally, red over green.

The badge of St. Helena, an island in the Atlantic, is a shield displaying

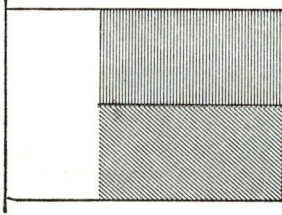

Malagasy Republic   St. Helena

an Indiaman, with sails furled and flying the St. George's Cross, approaching a passage between two peaks, one black and one brown.

The flag of Botswana, previously known as Bechuanaland, is a horizontal tricolour of blue, black fimbriated with white, and blue.

Two regions, though actually situated inside the Republic of South Africa, still belong to the Commonwealth. The flag of Swaziland is a horizontal tricolour, blue, red, and blue, with gold fimbriations; upon the central stripe are displayed a number of native weapons (Plate XIII, figure 6). That of Lesotho, formerly Basutoland, is blue with two vertical stripes, green and red, in the hoist; in the fly a native hat is shown in white.

Colonized both from Britain and from Holland, the former Union of South Africa was unified within what was then the British Empire only after the Boer War of 1899–1902. Its National Flag was the British Red Ensign, distinguished by a quartered shield in the fly displaying the emblems of the Union's four provinces: a white-robed female figure holding an anchor, the traditional symbol of hope, for Cape Colony with the Cape of Good Hope; two galloping wildebeeste for Natal; a flowering orange tree for the Orange River Colony (formerly the Orange Free State); and a Trek Waggon, one of those carts in which the early Dutch colonists journeyed into the unknown, for the Transvaal.

Badge of South Africa

This was not considered satisfactory, however, and after much discussion a new National Flag, which is also the Jack, was chosen in 1927. This is a horizontal tricolour; its colours, orange, white, and blue, are those of the

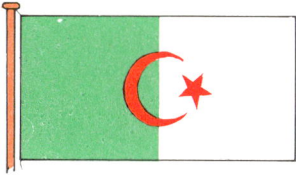

1. Algeria

2. Arab Republic of Egypt
(former flag)

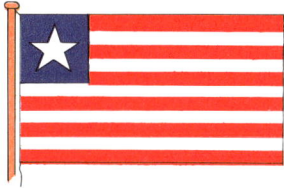

3. Liberia

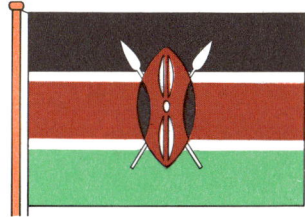

4. Kenya

5. Uganda

6. Swaziland

7. Tanzania

8. Republic of South Africa

Plate XIII

great Dutch liberator, William of Orange. In the centre of the white stripe
appear three smaller flags.

The central flag, shown as hanging vertically, represents the Orange Free
State; it bears seven horizontal stripes, alternately white and orange, and
also contains the modern Dutch
flag of red, white, and blue. On
the hoist side of this, spread
horizontally, is the Union Flag,
symbolizing the share which the
British took in the development
of South Africa. On the side
towards the fly, also spread hori-

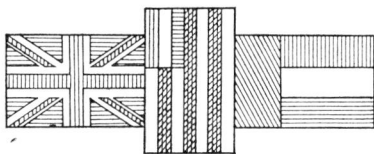

Republic of South Africa

zontally, is the old Transvaal *Vierkleur* (four colour) banner, the Dutch
flag with a broad green stripe in its hoist to represent 'Young Holland'. The
whole flag thus represents every European element in the region, the Dutch,
the British, and the Boer trekkers (Plate XIII, figure 8).

The Ensign of the South African Naval Forces places the National Flag
in the canton of a white flag bearing a broad dark-green cross of the St.
George type. The South African Air Force Ensign similarly places the
National Flag in the canton; its field is air force blue, and in the fly is a plan,
in dark blue edged with white, of the fort at Cape Town on which appears,
in orange, the emblem of a leaping springbok.

All these flags were retained when in 1961 the Union withdrew from the
British Commonwealth to become independent as the Republic of South
Africa.

The Transkei is the first of the regions which the South African Government is assigning as a 'Bantu Homeland' for its non-white peoples. It has its
own flag, which has to be flown in a position inferior to that of the South
African flag; it is a horizontal tricolour of ochre-red, white, and green.

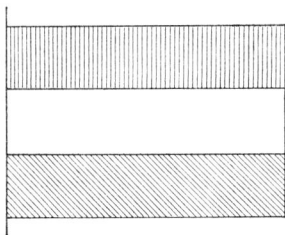

The Transkei

14

THE FLAGS OF AUSTRALASIA AND ANTARCTICA

Lift up an ensign to the nations from far

THE BIBLE

THE flags of Australia and New Zealand are neither heraldic nor do they represent any creature of earth; they are based on the southern sky.

The first explorers of the Antipodes were perplexed at finding strange beasts and birds, strange plants and trees, strange tribes with stranger customs and, most bewildering of all, a strange sky. They rejoiced to see in the midst of these unfamiliar constellations the emblem of their religion, a group of stars in the form of a cross; they may have regarded this as a sign from Heaven that they could not travel beyond the Divine care. When they realized that this group could be used, like the Pointers in the Great Bear, to indicate the Pole, their respect for it increased. No wonder, then, that this star-group, the Southern Cross, figures on coats of arms and flags.

Australia, though previously visited by European ships, was first systematically surveyed by the great English navigator and explorer, Captain James Cook. Since he first hoisted it at Botany Bay in 1770, the Union Flag has flown over the Continent. It now appears in the canton of the flags flown by the Commonwealth of Australia, which became a Federal Commonwealth in 1901. The arms of the Commonwealth, which form the field of the Personal Flag of Queen Elizabeth II for Australia, combine those of its six States as described below, and have an ermine border.

The Australian Ensigns bear in the fly a group of five stars, one smaller than the others, resembling those of the Southern Cross. In the hoist is a larger star, which corresponds to nothing in the sky and is purely symbolic: it is the Australian 'Commonwealth Star'. The stars are white, and except for the small star in the Cross, which is five-pointed, each has seven points (Plate XIV, figure 1).

Ships of the Royal Australian Navy fly a Blue Ensign of this type as a Jack; in 1921 they were given permission to fly the White Ensign at the stern. In 1967, however, that Navy adopted its own White Ensign, in which the St. George's Cross is replaced by the six stars of the National Flag with their colours reversed—blue on a white field. The Red Ensign is Australia's Merchant Flag, the Blue Ensign the National Flag. The Royal Australian Air Force and Australian Civil Air Ensigns combine the corresponding British Ensigns with the Commonwealth Star and the Southern Cross emblem.

Each of the six States in the Australian Commonwealth has its own badge, which appears in the fly of its ensign. That of Victoria consists of the five stars of the Southern Cross, white and surmounted by the Royal Crown in full colour on a blue field; this emblem, which dates from 1851, may have suggested that now used by the Australian Commonwealth. Four stars appear on the badge of New South Wales, but instead of representing the Southern Cross they are arranged symmetrically on the arms of a red

Australia
Personal Flag of Queen Elizabeth II

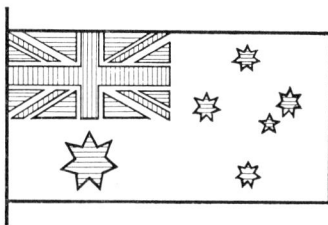

Ensign of the
Royal Australian Navy

St. George's Cross; at its centre is a lion similar to those of the Royal Standard; this, like the stars, is gold. The English lion, in red, forms the badge of Tasmania. That of Queensland is a blue Maltese Cross with the Royal Crown at its centre. All three of these badges are heraldic and all appear on white fields.

Two badges show, black on yellow fields, characteristic Australian birds. That of South Australia is the white-backed piping shrike, *displayed* as the Heralds say (with its wings outspread) but gripping a red and green perch. That of Western Australia greatly astonished the naturalists when it was discovered: it is the famous black swan.

New Zealand is not part of the Australian Commonwealth. It became a Dominion in 1907. Its arms include four white-bordered red stars on a blue field; a gold fleece on red; a gold wheatsheaf on red; two hammers, gold on blue; and three ships black on white—this design forms the field of the Personal Flag of Queen Elizabeth II for New Zealand.

The earliest flag of New Zealand, dating from 1834 and chosen out of three designs by the Maori Chiefs, is now used as a House Flag by a shipping

New Zealand
Personal Flag of Queen Elizabeth II

company: a St. George's Cross and four white stars on blue placed in the canton of another St. George's Cross (Plate VI, figure 4).

The emblem of New Zealand is now the Southern Cross, but in a simpler form than that of Australia: four stars in the fly of its ensigns. Those on its

Queensland

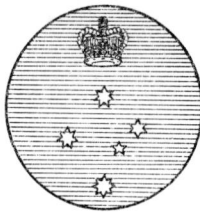

Victoria

New South Wales

South Australia

Tasmania

Western Australia

National Flag, the Blue Ensign, are red with a white fimbriation; the miniature of the National Flag is used as the Jack of the Royal New Zealand Navy. This, in 1968, adopted a new White Ensign, with the British Union Flag in the canton and four red stars representing the Southern Cross in the fly. The stars on its Red Ensign, its Merchant Flag, are white (Plate XIV, figure 2).

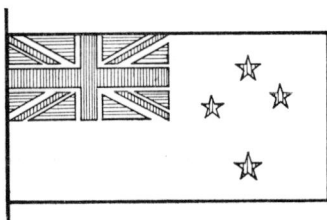

Ensign of the
Royal New Zealand Navy

The Royal New Zealand Air Force Ensign is similar to the R.A.F. Ensign but places the letters 'N.Z.' in white on the red central disc. The New Zealand Civil Air Ensign displays the Southern Cross, in red, in the fourth quarter of a flag otherwise resembling the British Civil Air Ensign.

Until recently the official flag of Papua New Guinea, which is at present administered by Australia, was the National Flag of that Commonwealth. The flags displayed at sea are the Blue and the Red Ensign. The country is scheduled to become independent in the near future, however, and meantime its own flag may be used alone or with the Australian National Flag, the latter being given precedence.

The new flag is divided diagonally. Its lower half, in the hoist, shows the Southern Cross, white on black, to indicate the relations of the country with Australia; its upper half, in the fly, displays a bird of paradise, yellow on a red field (Plate XIV, figure 5). Red and black were chosen as the predominant colours because of their widespread use in native art.

Many of the islands in Oceania are within the Commonwealth and some are administered by the Western Pacific High Commissioner, who places the initials 'W.P.H.C.' below the Imperial Crown in red and gold on a white field surrounded by a garland at the centre of the Union Flag. Another badge similarly consists of this Crown with letters or words in black: the crown on a white circle in the fly of the Blue Ensign with the addition of the words NEW HEBRIDES forms the flag of the Resident Commissioner of that group of islands. The French tricolour and the Union Jack are also flown here, side by side, as the New Hebrides are administered as an Anglo-French Condominium. Some of the islands place their own badges on the Union Flag and the Blue Ensign. That of the British Solomon Islands Protectorate includes a lion, gold on red; an eagle, a turtle, native weapons, and two birds, on a blue-and-white shield.

Western Pacific
High Commissioner

New Hebrides

The badge of the Gilbert and Ellice Islands shows a frigate bird flying over the sea from which the sun is rising; bird and sun are gold, the sky red, and the sea blue and white (Plate XIV, figure 8).

The small island of Nauru, a special member of the Commonwealth, indicates its position just south of the Equator, by a large white star just below a horizontal yellow stripe on a blue field representing the sea.

British Solomon Islands
Protectorate

Gilbert and Ellice
Islands

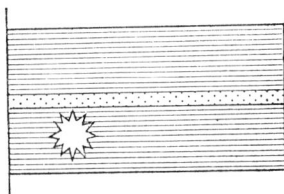

Nauru

The State Flag of the Kingdom of Tonga, formerly known as the Tongan or Friendly Islands, is a Red Ensign; in the canton is not the Union Flag but a red Greek Cross (with equal arms) on a white field, reversing the Swiss Flag (Plate XIV, figure 6). The King's Standard places the red

Greek Cross on a six-pointed white star at the centre of a quartered flag
with a very striking design: in the first quarter are three white stars on a

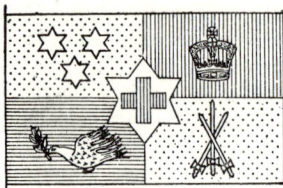

Standard of H.M. King of
Tonga

yellow field, in the second a gold crown on
a red field, in the third a dove with an olive-
spray in its mouth, white on blue; in the
fourth three crossed swords, white on a
yellow field.

Now that Fiji is independent within the
Commonwealth it uses as its National Flag
the British Blue Ensign, but with an azure
field. On this appears the shield from the
island's coat of arms, which also distinguishes
its other Ensigns, and which illustrates the island's products. The top of
the shield displays the Lion of England holding a native emblem, a coco-pod,
gold on a red field: the lower part of the shield is quartered by a St. George's
Cross; in its quarters are three sugar-canes, a coconut palm, a dove with an
olive-spray in its beak, and a bunch of bananas (Plate XIV, figure 7).

Samoa, the Navigators' Islands, consists of two main groups. The greater
part of the islands, Western Samoa, became in 1962 the first independent
Polynesian State; its flag is red with a blue canton displaying the Southern
Cross (Plate XIV, figure 3).

The islands further east form American Samoa. Its flag is blue, with a
white triangle, bordered with red, its apex in the centre of the hoist and its
base along the fly. Upon the triangle an eagle symbolizing American
protection grasps native emblems of authority and culture (Plate XIV,
figure 4).

The United States controls several islands in the Pacific. The flag of
Guam is dark blue with a red border; in its centre is an ellipse, on which
appears a river scene with a canoe and a coconut tree, together with the
word 'GUAM'.

Guam

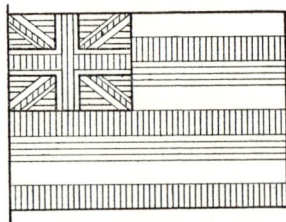

Hawaii

The islands of Hawaii, although now one of the United States, still fly
the flag which they used while independent in the nineteenth century. The
flag is crossed by eight horizontal stripes of white, red, and blue, representing

FLAGS OF AUSTRALASIA AND ANTARCTICA

1. Australia

2. New Zealand

3. Western Samoa

4. American Samoa

5. Papua New Guinea

6. Tonga

7. Fiji

8. Gilbert and Ellice Islands

9. British Antarctic Survey Work

Plate XIV

the principal islands of the group: in the canton is the emblem not of the States but of Britain—the Union Flag.

The South Pacific Commission includes representatives of Australia, Fiji, France, Nauru, New Zealand, the United Kingdom, the United States, and Western Samoa. Its flag is blue and bears a broken circle symbolizing an atoll, a stylized palm tree, and eight stars, all in white: the six-pointed stars are in token of the member States.

The Continent of Antarctica is divided into seven sectors. Sovereignty claims to these are frozen, however, by the terms of

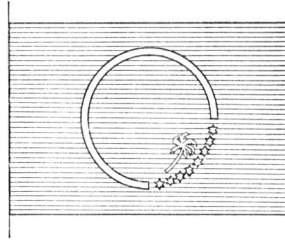

South Pacific Commission

the Antarctic Treaty, and research parties fly their own National Flag whichever sector they may be in. Vessels of the National Environment Research Council, when engaged on British Antarctic Survey Work, fly a Blue Ensign displaying a badge similar to that formerly used by the Falkland Islands Dependencies: a torch, symbolizing knowledge, appears on a red triangle upon a shield, white below and white crossed with blue wavy lines above, to represent the icefields and the sea (Plate XIV, figure 9).

15

INTERNATIONAL FLAGS

Nation shall speak peace unto nation.

THE OLD MOTTO OF THE B.B.C.

NATIONS, shipping-lines and public services are not the only organizations which use flags. Any group of people, working together in a common cause, may devise an emblem for use not only as a badge but as a banner. Captain Scott and his comrades, when they made their heroic dash to the South Pole, had their own Sledge Flag: it hangs today among the regimental colours on the walls of Exeter Cathedral.

So customary is the use of flags that they have even passed into legend. A Fairy Flag is treasured in a Scottish castle, and the story-tellers of old imagined that Fairyland had its own flag—a gold unicorn rampant on a green field.

Some flags, instead of being national, are intended to help the people of all nations to co-operate for the common good. The most important of these form the code which enables any two ships to communicate with one another, no matter the country they hail from or the language their crews speak.

One of the first codes used by merchant ships was devised in 1817 by Captain Marryat, famous as the author of many exciting sea stories. Basing it on the code used by the Royal Navy, he had to alter it greatly to omit the flag-hoists which gave battle orders, and to devise new ones dealing with trade. He had also to transform a code whose purpose was secrecy into one intended to be universally understood.

Captain Marryat's code used flags, representing the figures 1 to 9 and 0, two special flags and four special pendants. Successful though it was, the number of different hoists it provided was inadequate, and in 1857 it was replaced by a new code prepared by the British Board of Trade. This—the first International Code—used eighteen flags: instead of numbers, each represented a letter of the alphabet. No vowels were included, however, lest their inclusion should make some of the hoists spell swear-words in this language or that.

Its eighteen flags again proved insufficient for the number of messages needed, and a revised code provided a flag for every letter of the alphabet. This made possible thousands of additional hoists, and also enabled words and names not in the code to be spelled out (the difficulty about swear-words was easily overcome by using common sense in drawing up the code).

This revised code was in use until 1969; the new International Code

106

of Signals, in use today, is based on the principle that each signal has a complete meaning. The old 'vocabulary' method (spelling out words letter by letter) is no longer used, except for the names of vessels and places.

There are twenty-six flags (including two burgees) for the letters of the alphabet, and ten pendants for the figures 1 to 9 and 0. There is also a special Code and Answering Pendant and three triangular Substitute Flags to avoid the need to have extra flags when the same letter or figure occurs more than once in a group. This Code can be transmitted by all means of communication, including radiotelephony and radiotelegraphy, and some single-letter signals can be made by a flashing light or by sound—for example on a ship's whistle.

Single-letter signals are used for messages of importance, urgency, or which are in very common use. Thus flag A, which formerly showed that the vessel flying it was on a speed-trial, now means 'I have a diver down; keep well clear at slow speed'; B, a red burgee, shows that a vessel is carrying, loading or unloading dangerous goods; U means 'You are running into danger', O means 'Man Overboard'; and so forth. One signal flag is famous: the Blue Peter (flag P), announcing that the ship flying it is 'About to Sail'.

Hoists of two flags are signals of distress or warning or deal with the handling of ships: thus NC is the Distress Signal, 'I want immediate assistance'. There are also hoists of three flags, one number being flown below two letters to show variations in the meaning of the basic signals; signals with the flags XT refer to weather expected, and XT1 means 'Weather expected is good'.

Hoists of three flags, headed by M, are concerned with medical matters, and can be used to describe symptoms and prescribe treatment in cases of sudden illness at sea: MPF means 'Patient is improving' and MPP (really MP and Substitute Flag 2) means 'Treatment has been effective'.

Latitude and longitude are shown by four Numerical Pendants below the flags L or G respectively, and other flags above the pendants indicate date, distance, speed, or time. Names and words not in the code can be spelled out letter by letter, the special signal YZ being made previously to show when the spelling begins.

A vessel wishing to signal by the International Code begins (unless she is addressing all ships within visual signalling distance) by hoisting the flags which indicate the name of the ship she is signalling to and follows this by the first hoist of the message. The ship to which the signal is sent hoists the Code and Answering Pendant at the dip (some distance below the mast-head). As soon as the message is understood the Pendant is raised to the mast-head, returning to the dip when the ship sending the message lowers her flags. The other hoists are raised and acknowledged in the same way. Finally the sending ship hoists her Code Pendant to show that the message is complete, and the receiving ship again raises her Pendant to the mast-head to show that this too is understood.

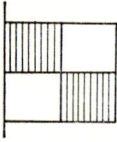

U
You are Running
into Danger

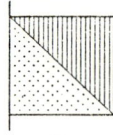

O
Man Overboard

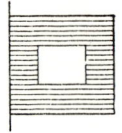

P
Blue Peter
About to Sail

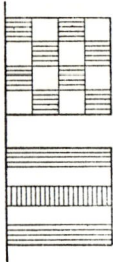

NC
Distress Signal

YZ
Words Following
are in Plain
Language

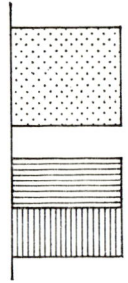

QE
I Have Headway

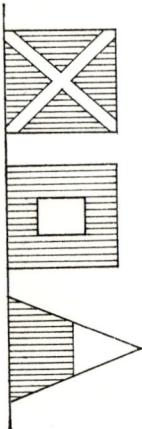

MPP
Treatment Has Been
Effective

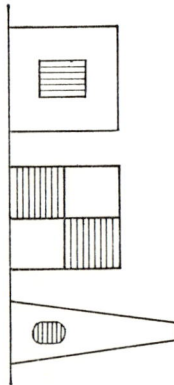

SU1
My Cargo is Coal

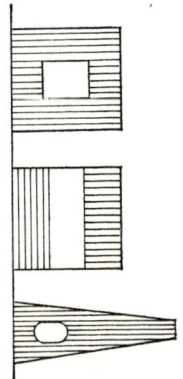

PT2
The Tide is Falling

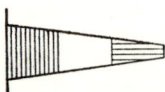

Numerical Pendant
3

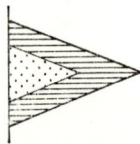

First Substitute

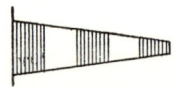

Code and Answering
Pendant

A ship of the Royal Navy when signalling to a merchant vessel keeps her Code Pendant hoisted conspicuously to show that she is using not a special naval code but the International Code.

The very simple Fisherman's Code has virtually fallen into disuse as urgent messages between fishing vessels and cruisers employed on Fishery Duty in the North Sea can be carried out by radio-telephony or by loud hailer. By international agreement of the countries concerned, vessels employed on Fishery Duty fly a pendant quartered blue and yellow.

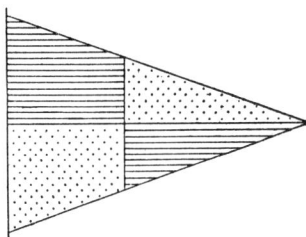

North Sea Fishery Duty

From a distance the different flags are hard to distinguish, and the emergency distress signal formed by flying an ensign upside down is therefore no longer used. There are eleven distress signals which can be recognized from afar; one is a ball hoisted above or below a square flag.

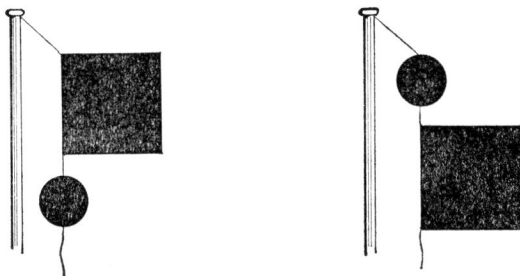

Distress Signals

Another warning recognizable from a distance is the Storm Signal, hoisted in bad weather at many of our ports. A cone hoisted point downwards means that a storm is approaching from the south; one with its point upwards, from the north. Three red balls hoisted one above the other give warning that a port is closed to shipping.

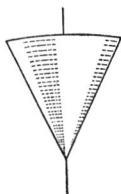

South Cone

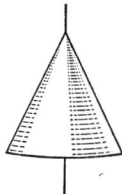

North Cone

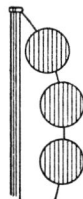

Port Closed

Although the wireless enables messages to be sent more quickly, in far greater detail, and over far greater distances than signal flags, it has not put the International Code out of use. Not only are the flags simpler and less liable to go wrong than complicated electrical apparatus: they are international while wireless messages, in clear, whether by morse or spoken by radio, can be understood only by those who know the language in which they are sent, though of course, a few morse signals such as the well-known call for help, 'S.O.S.', are understood almost everywhere.

So great is this advantage that many attempts have been made to introduce an international language, to be used, as the code flags are used, by all nations. Of the many synthetic languages invented for this purpose, the

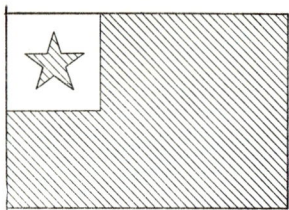
Esperanto

most popular is Esperanto, thanks not only to its merits but to the zeal of the Esperantists. They have their own flag, flown over their conferences and offices: a five-pointed green star (the colour and emblem of hope —the word Esperanto means 'hopeful'), its points representing the five continents, in the white canton of an ensign with a green fly.

One aim of the international language is world peace. Attempts to bring this about have also been made by organizations aiming at promoting goodwill between the nations. The best known of these movements is the Scout Association, which was founded in 1908 by Lord Baden-Powell of

Scout Flag

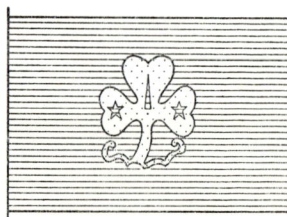
Girl Guide and Girl Scout Flag

Gilwell, and which is active in many lands. The World Scout Flag shows the fleur-de-lis badge in white on a purple field. The flag of the World Association of Girl Guides and Girl Scouts bears the trefoil badge, yellow on a blue field.

One international flag stands for a more immediate ideal: instead of seeking world peace, it tries to reduce the horrors of war. In 1863 an international conference drew up rules for aiding the sick and wounded of warring nations and for protecting those who tended them and the buildings which housed them. Needing a flag to fly over hospitals and dressing-stations, the conference, having met in Geneva, used the Swiss flag with its colours reversed: a Greek Cross, red on a white field, is the famous Red Cross (Plate XV, figure 3). (Moslem countries, however, use the Crescent, red on a white field (Plate XV, figure 4), and Iran has a special Hospital Flag, displaying the Lion and Sun, also red on white (Plate XV, figure 5).

The most earnest attempts to bring about world peace have been made by the Christian Churches. Just as the Moslem emblem, the crescent and star, appears on many Eastern flags, so the Christian emblem, the Cross, appears on many of the flags of Christendom. The Roman Catholic Church, the headquarters of which forms an independent sovereign state, the Vatican City in Rome, has moreover its own flag, used by its members all over the world—in London this flag sometimes flies over Westminster Cathedral.

In the Middle Ages the Pope, besides being the head of the Roman Catholic Church, was also ruler of a country in central Italy, the Papal States; during the nineteenth century these were merged into the newly formed Italian nation. Soon after the First World War, however, a small area in the heart of Rome regained its independence under the name of Vatican City.

This restored to use, with slight alterations, the former Papal Flag. It is halved vertically, yellow in the hoist, white in the fly; on the white half are the Papal Arms, the Triple Crown above two crossed keys, yellow and white. This, of course, breaks the heraldic rules, by bringing the two metals, gold and silver, together with no colour to separate them; it does this not by accident but deliberately, to show that the Church is not bound by such rules (Plate XV, figure 2).

In addition to the Church of England flags—the Diocesan emblem in the canton of a St. George's Cross—other Protestant Churches possess their own flags. A few religious bodies have their own ships and consequently need their own House Flags. The 'Flying Angel', white on a blue field, is the flag of the Missions to Seamen. The Dove, also white on a blue field, is that of the London Missionary Society. Similarly the Salvation Army, which makes use of military methods, has its own colours, the 'Blood and Fire' flag.

In the summer of 1948 the flags of many nations were unfurled over London, and in the midst of them there was another banner. This was the Olympic Flag, the emblem of the Olympic Games, an international competition in many varied sporting events which in normal times is held every four years in one or other of the world's capitals. It consists of a chain of five interlinked rings, each of a different colour, on a white field (Plate XV, figure 6).

The chain, an ancient symbol of unity and co-operation, was intended to represent the five continents of the world linked in unbroken friendship.

One idea of the colours of the links was that each represented one of the continents—blue for Europe, yellow for Asia, black for Africa, green for America, and red for Australasia. Although yellow and black are not bad emblems of Asia and Africa, however, it is difficult to see how the other colours were arrived at. It is much more likely that the five colours were chosen because they are those used in almost all the world's national flags.

There is a whole code of flags for use in motor competitions. Here, as elsewhere, a red flag is the sign of danger, and commands a complete and immediate stop. A yellow flag is the warning that care must be taken; waved, it tells the motorist to be prepared to stop. A yellow flag striped vertically with red is a warning of spilt oil. A blue flag means that a competitor is being closely followed or overtaken, a white flag that an ambulance or service car is on the circuit. One car can be ordered to stop on its next round by a black flag bearing its number. The end of the race is signalized by a flag chequered in black and white.

Several attempts have been made to design a world flag, which should be the emblem not of one nation or religious body but of all mankind. The League of Nations Union used a flag showing a map of the world. It is, of course, impossible to represent the globe on a flat surface without deforming the shapes of the countries. The L.N.U. chose what is known as the Equivalent Projection, which represents the world as a flattened oval, twice as broad as it is high; this has the advantage that though it badly deforms the shapes of the countries it represents their correct relative sizes.

The United Nations Organization, formed after the Second World War, also shows a world map on its flag. (An earlier flag, showing four red bars, vertical on a white field, to represent the 'Four Freedoms', was not official and was never adopted.) Its map, however, is different, showing the continents grouped round the North Pole. The land areas, the signs of latitude and longitude, and the wreath which surrounds the map, are white on a sky-blue field (Plate XV, figure 1).

Other international organizations also have their own emblems. For example, the flag of the North Atlantic Treaty Organization (N.A.T.O.) is dark blue, and displays, in white, within a white circle symbolizing unity, the emblem of the Compass Rose, to show that the nations of the Atlantic Alliance are steering towards world peace. Blue and white are the Organization's colours, and the blue also represents the Atlantic Ocean (Plate XV, figure 7).

The South-East Asia Treaty Organization (S.E.A.T.O.) also uses a blue flag; the white shield at its centre displays in outline a world globe, with its south-eastern quadrant shaded blue, and upon this appears, in gold, the olive branch, the traditional symbol of peace (Plate XV, figure 8).

INTERNATIONAL FLAGS

1. United Nations

2. Vatican City

3. Red Cross

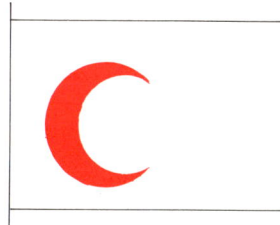

4. Red Crescent

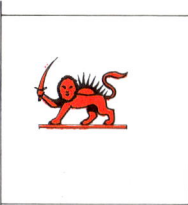

5. Red Lion and Sun Society

6. Olympic Flag

7. N.A.T.O.

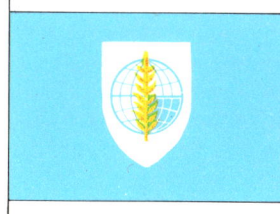

8. S.E.A.T.O.

Plate XV

APPENDIX 1

From 8 a.m. till Sunset

6 February	Her Majesty's Accession.
19 February	Birthday of the Prince Andrew.
1 March	St. David's Day. [*See* Note 1.(*a*)]
10 March	Birthday of the Prince Edward.
31 March	Birthday of the Duke of Gloucester.
21 April	Birthday of Her Majesty the Queen.
23 April	St. George's Day. [*See* Note 1.(*b*)]
2 June	Coronation Day.
June (as appointed)	Official Celebration of Her Majesty's Birthday; Commonwealth Day.
10 June	Birthday of the Duke of Edinburgh.
4 August	Birthday of Her Majesty Queen Elizabeth the Queen Mother.
15 August	Birthday of the Princess Anne.
21 August	Birthday of the Princess Margaret.
November	Remembrance Day. [*See* Note 2.]
14 November	Birthday of the Prince of Wales.
20 November	Her Majesty's Wedding Day.
30 November	St. Andrew's Day. [*See* Note 1.(*c*)]

ALSO: The day of the opening of a Session of the Houses of Parliament by Her Majesty. [*See* Note 3.]

The day of the prorogation of a Session of the Houses of Parliament by Her Majesty. [*See* Note 3.]

NOTES

1.(*a*) Flags should be flown on this day in Wales only.

(*b*) Flags should be flown on this day in England only.

(*c*) Flags should be flown on this day in Scotland only.

Where a building has two or more flagstaffs the appropriate National Flag may be flown in addition to the Union Jack but not in a superior position.

2. Remembrance Day is the second Sunday in November. Flags should be flown right up all day.

3. Flags should be flown on this day irrespective of whether or not Her Majesty performs the ceremony in person, but only from buildings in the Greater London area.

4. The Royal Standard is never hoisted when Her Majesty is passing in procession; if the Queen is to be present in a building, instructions should be sought through the Department of the Environment [Special Services Secretariat 2b].

Crown Copyright Reserved
Reproduced by Permission of the Department of the Environment

APPENDIX 2

RULES FOR HOISTING FLAGS ON GOVERNMENT BUILDINGS

*The following Regulations are circulated by Her Majesty's Command
to the Government Offices concerned*

Dates on which Flags are to be Flown

The dates named in Appendix 1.

The only additions to these dates will be those which are notified to
the Department of the Environment by Her Majesty's Command, and
they will be communicated by the Department of the Environment to
the other Departments.

Provincial Buildings

The Schedule as given in Appendix 1 applies to provincial as well as to
London buildings (but see Notes 1 and 3 in Appendix 1); where it has been
the practice—as in the case of some Custom Houses—to fly the flag daily,
that practice may continue.

Occasions on which Flags are to be Flown at Half-Mast

(*a*) From the announcement of the death up to the funeral of the
Sovereign, except on Proclamation Day, when they are hoisted right up
from 11 a.m. to sunset.

(*b*) The funerals of members of the Royal Family, subject to special
commands from Her Majesty in each case.

(*c*) The funerals of Foreign Rulers, subject to special commands from
Her Majesty in each case.

(*d*) The funerals of Prime Ministers and Ex-Prime Ministers of the
United Kingdom.

(*e*) Other occasions by special command of Her Majesty which will be
communicated by the Department of the Environment to other Departments.

Rules when Days for flying Flags coincide with Days for flying Flags at Half-Mast

To be flown—

(*a*) although a member of the Royal Family, or a near relative of the
Royal Family, may be lying dead, unless special commands be received
from Her Majesty to the contrary;

(*b*) although it may be the day of the funeral of a Foreign Ruler.

If the body of a very distinguished subject is lying at a Government
Office the flag may fly at half-mast on that office until the body has left
(provided it is a day on which the flag would fly) and then the flag is to
be hoisted right up. On all other Public Buildings the flag will fly as usual.

APPENDIX 3

Royal Standard

Whenever Her Majesty is in the Abbey or Precincts and when she opens or prorogues Parliament in person.

St. Peter's Flag

On all Church festivals, being the Patron Saint.

Abbey Flag

On Ascension Day, Coronation Day, the Queen's Birthday and Wedding Day (the Queen being the Visitor of the Abbey),[1] and the Birthdays of the other members of the Royal Family. It is also flown on feast days associated with Edward the Confessor, the Founder, and on other occasions of local importance and significance.

The Union Flag

On Commonwealth Day and Remembrance Sunday.

The Flags of St. George, St. Andrew, St. Patrick, and St. David on their respective days.

R.A.F. Flag

On Battle of Britain Sunday.

The Flags of the Commonwealth Countries

On their respective Foundation or Independence Days. There are stalls in the choir for the High Commissioners, as the Abbey has special links with the Commonwealth.

[1] In cathedrals the Visitor is the Bishop of the Diocese.

115

INDEX